The MAILBOX®
The Education Center®

Seas STORYTIME

MW01267692

Picture book activities for every season and these curriculum areas!

- Literacy
- Math
- Art
- Science
- Speaking
- Listening
- Social Studies
- Music
- Movement

50 different books!

Managing Editors: Kimberly Brugger-Murphy, Brenda Miner

Editorial Team: Becky S. Andrews, Randi Austin, Diane Badden, Janet Boyce, Kimberley Bruck, Karen A. Brudnak, Kitty Campbell, Pam Crane, Kathryn Davenport, Roxanne LaBell Dearman, Lynette Dickerson, Cherie Durbin, Sue Fleischmann, Sarah Foreman, Deborah Garmon, Ada Goren, Heather E. Graley, Tazmen Hansen, Marsha Heim, Lori Z. Henry, Lucia Kemp Henry, Debra Liverman, Coramarie Marinan, Dorothy C. McKinney, Thad H. McLaurin, Sharon Murphy, Jennifer Nunn, Tina Petersen, Mark Rainey, Greg D. Rieves, Kelly Robertson, Hope Rodgers, Rebecca Saunders, Barry Slate, Leanne Stratton Swinson, Donna K. Teal, Joshua Thomas, Carole Watkins, Zane Williard

www.themailbox.com

©2009 The Mailbox® Books
All rights reserved.
ISBN10 #1-56234-861-2 • ISBN13 #978-156234-861-8

Manufactured in the United States
10 9 8 7 6 5 4 3 2 1

Table of Contents

What's Inside 3

Fall

The Kissing Hand 4

Froggy Goes to School....................... 6

Off to School, Baby Duck! 8

Brown Bear, Brown Bear, What Do
You See? 10

Ten Apples Up On Top!....................... 12

The Apple Pie Tree............................ 14

Nuts to You!...................................... 16

It's Pumpkin Time!............................. 18

Red Leaf, Yellow Leaf......................... 20

Go Away, Big Green Monster! 22

The Little Old Lady Who Was Not Afraid
of Anything 24

A Turkey for Thanksgiving 26

I Know an Old Lady Who Swallowed a Pie ... 28

Winter

The Jacket I Wear in the Snow............. 30

The Mitten... 32

The Hat.. 34

Bear Snores On.................................. 36

Gingerbread Baby 38

The Snowy Day 40

Snowballs 42

Snowmen at Night 44

Hanukkah Lights, Hanukkah Nights 46

The Night Before Christmas 48

The Polar Express 50

Kente Colors...................................... 52

Happy Birthday, Martin Luther King............. 54

Substitute Groundhog................................. 56

Guess How Much I Love You 58

Roses Are Pink, Your Feet Really Stink 60

Spring

Big Red Barn 62

We're Going on a Bear Hunt 64

Growing Vegetable Soup............................ 66

Tops & Bottoms 68

The Grouchy Ladybug 70

Jump, Frog, Jump!..................................... 72

In the Small, Small Pond 74

Mrs. Wishy-Washy..................................... 76

One Duck Stuck... 78

The Very Hungry Caterpillar 80

Waiting for Wings 82

Green Eggs and Ham................................. 84

The Golden Egg Book 86

Summer

One Hot Summer Day 88

Jamberry... 90

The Little Mouse, the Red Ripe Strawberry,
and the Big Hungry Bear........................ 92

Blueberries for Sal 94

Down by the Bay 96

Fish Eyes: A Book You Can Count On 98

Swimmy 100

A House for Hermit Crab 102

Patterns and Reproducibles................... 104

What's Inside

200 activities to use with **50** different picture books!

Each picture book unit includes

A brief description of the book

A large cover illustration

A Seasonal Link

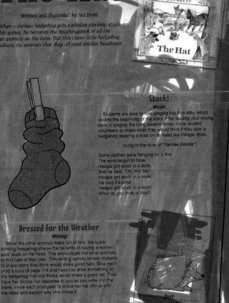

Four fun and creative activities

Look for timesaving patterns and reproducibles too!

The Kissing Hand

Written by Audrey Penn
Illustrated by Ruth E. Harper and Nancy M. Leak

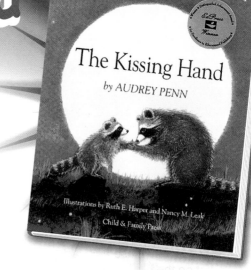

Chester Raccoon needs reassurance as he heads off to school for the very first time. So his mother shows him a secret way to remember her love, even while he's away from her.

I need a kissing hand!

Emily

My Kissing Hand

Speaking

In this heartfelt story, Mrs. Raccoon's secret kissing hand gives Chester the strength and reassurance he needs when he feels afraid to go to school. Your little ones will get the reassurance they need with a kissing hand of their own. Post a daily schedule on a wall. Give each child a hand cutout labeled with the words "I need a kissing hand!" Have her write her name on her cutout. Review the daily schedule with your students. Invite each child to comment on any events that may make her feel unsure; then have her post her cutout near the event on the schedule. Use the hands as a reminder throughout the day to give extra support and reassurance when needed.

Kissing Hand Magnet

Art

Youngsters will be eager to give parents these magnets which are reminiscent of the little raccoon's kissing hand. Trace each child's hand on craft foam; then cut out the tracing. Have the child use craft glue to attach a craft foam heart to the middle of her hand cutout. Instruct her to attach a magnetic strip to one side of a spring-style clothespin; then glue the cutout to the other side. These magnets are perfect for holding youngsters' masterpieces.

Night School
Science

Chester goes to school in the nighttime instead of the daytime. Spotlight Chester's nocturnal nature with this artwork. Revisit the page that shows Chester going to school at night. Explain that raccoons are nocturnal animals—they sleep during the day and are awake at night. Next, have each child cut out a gray construction paper copy of the raccoon pattern on page 104. Then have him spread black fingerpaint on a sheet of finger-paint paper. Have him use an eyedropper to drip yellow paint on the black paint to make stars. Finally, have the child press the raccoon cutout into the wet paint.

Fireflies
Math

The nocturnal schoolyard in this story shines with a sky filled with fireflies! Help youngsters count the fireflies on the pages picturing the treetop classroom toward the end of the book. Then invite little ones to do some hands-on counting with this simple idea. Give each child a sheet of black construction paper and a supply of yellow pom-poms (fireflies). Hold up a number card and have students identify the number. Then instruct each child to place the corre-sponding number of fireflies on her paper. After checking for accuracy, have young-sters remove the fireflies. Continue in the same manner with other number cards.

Froggy Goes to School

Written by Jonathan London
Illustrated by Frank Remkiewicz

Froggy has a dream that he shows up for the first day of school wearing only his underwear! Fortunately, the reality of his first school day is much better than his dream.

Summer Fun
Speaking

In this back-to-school story, Froggy can hardly wait to tell his classmates what he did over the summer. Your youngsters will be eager to talk about their summer adventures as well with this fun circle-time activity! Draw large eyes on a green ball so it resembles a frog. Gently bounce the ball to a child as you lead the group in saying Froggy's chant: "Bubble, bubble, toot, toot. Chicken, airplane, soldier." Encourage the youngster to talk about something she did over the summer; then have her gently bounce the ball to a classmate as you lead the group in repeating the chant.

A Hungry Frog
Art

With this activity, youngsters make a fly-loving frog—just like Froggy in the story! Give each child a pink paper plate folded in half. Instruct him to paint the back of the plate green. After the paint dries, have him attach eye cutouts to the plate. Then have him glue a tongue cutout along the inside fold as shown. Finally, invite him to glue a small black pom-pom to the frog's tongue so it resembles a fly.

Flop, Flop, Flop
Math

Little ones will have fun hopping like Froggy with this cute counting idea! Label each of several frog cutouts with a different number and a corresponding dot set; then place the frogs in a backpack. Invite a child to pick a frog. Help her identify the number; then instruct her to hop like Froggy the appropriate number of times as you lead the group in counting aloud. After she is finished hopping, have her return the frog to the backpack. Continue in the same manner with each remaining child.

Fly Topping!
Fine motor

Froggy's breakfast is a delicious bowl of flies with milk. Your youngsters are sure to enjoy this super snack made with yummy imitation flies! Give each child a bowl of cereal. Provide a supply of mini chocolate chips (flies) along with several pairs of plastic tweezers. Encourage each child to use a pair of tweezers to pick up several chocolate chips and place them on his cereal. Help him pour milk into the bowl; then invite him to eat his delicious snack of cereal topped with flies!

Off to School, Baby Duck!

Written by Amy Hest
Illustrated by Jill Barton

It was the first day of school for Baby Duck, who was more nervous than excited to go. So Grandpa Duck waited for her at the schoolyard, knowing just the right questions to ask to make Baby Duck's worries disappear.

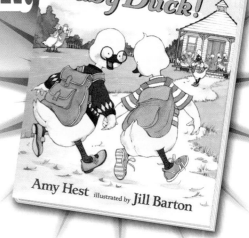

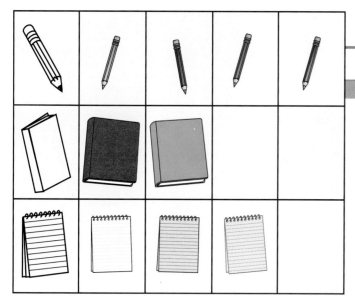

One Ducky Graph!
Math

In this delightful story, Baby Duck loved her school bag and all the important things inside. Your youngsters also are sure to have fun using this class backpack in a hands-on graphing activity! To prepare, place several pencils, books, and notepads in a backpack. Draw a graph, similar to the one shown, on a length of bulletin board paper and place it in your circle-time area. In turn, have each child remove an item from the backpack and place it in the appropriate column on the graph. Then lead youngsters in counting and comparing the number of school supplies in each column.

Baby Duck
Art

With this activity, little ones make a baby duck—just like Baby Duck in the story! Trace each child's shoe on yellow construction paper; then have her cut out the tracing. Cut a red pipe cleaner in half and bend one half so it resembles Baby Duck's glasses. Instruct the student to glue the glasses to the small end of the shoe cutout. Next, have her glue an orange paper beak cutout below the glasses and two yellow craft feathers to either side of the body for wings. Help her bend the remaining pipe cleaner half to make the duck's legs; then shape the ends so they resemble the duck's feet. Finally, have her glue the legs in place to the back of the cutout. After the glue is dry, encourage her to use a marker to make dot eyes.

Off to School, Baby Duck!

Fall

School Is Fun!
Music

Baby Duck is very nervous on her first day of school. Have little ones sing this tune to reassure Baby Duck that all will turn out well.

(sung to the tune of "If You're Happy and You Know It")

Oh, Baby Duck, don't worry. School is fun! (It's fun!)
Oh, Baby Duck, don't worry. School is fun! (It's fun!)
You'll make friends. Now aren't you lucky?
So be happy, Baby Ducky!
Oh, Baby Duck, don't worry. School is fun! (It's fun!)

First-Day Jitters
Literacy

On the morning of her first day of school, Baby Duck's stomach was all jittery! With this activity, youngsters can explain how they felt on the morning of their first day of school. Post an oversize schoolhouse cutout in your large-group area. Invite each child to describe how he felt on the morning of his first day of school. Then have him describe how he felt as the day went on. Record each student's response on the schoolhouse. After each child has had a turn, compare youngsters' comments to see how many students shared similar feelings.

Josh—I was scared because I didn't know anybody. But then I made a friend!

Maria—I was sad because I missed my mommy.

James—I was mad because I wanted my toys. But I liked the toys here!

Brown Bear, Brown Bear, What Do You See?

Written by Bill Martin Jr.
Illustrated by Eric Carle

Colorful critters traipse across the pages of this beloved book. The author's engaging and predictable text, along with the illustrator's large colorful collages, invites listeners to join in the fun!

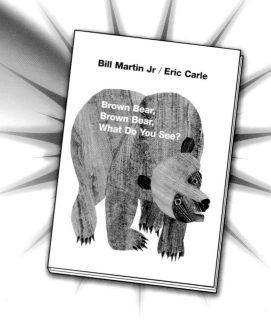

[Cole], [Cole], what do you see?
I see [a small black kitten] looking at me.

Children, Children, What Do You See?

Literacy

With this activity, youngsters use descriptive language to create a class book in a style similar to *Brown Bear, Brown Bear, What Do You See?* Give each child a sheet of paper programmed as shown. Have her write her name in the blank spaces in the first line. Next, instruct her to cut a desired picture from a magazine and glue it to the page. Encourage her to describe her picture using size, shape, or color words; then record her dictation on the remaining line. Bind the finished pages together between two covers with the title "Children, Children, What Do You See?"

Brown Bear

Art

With this activity, youngsters make a brown bear—just like the brown bear in the book! Mix together brown tempera paint, pencil shavings, and a small amount of glue to make textured paint. Invite each child to use the mixture to paint a sheet of white construction paper. After the paint is dry, cut a bear shape from the paper.

Brown Bear, Brown Bear, What Do You See?

Fall

Colorful Clues
Literacy

A rainbow of colorful animals parades across the pages of this engaging book. After several readings, challenge students to identify each animal according to its color with this fun game of colorful clues! Secretly choose an animal from a book page. Provide several clues to help youngsters identify the animal by naming other objects that are the same color. For example, you might say, "The animal on this page is the same color as broccoli and grass." After the animal is correctly identified, reveal the book page. Repeat the activity in the same manner as time allows.

It's the frog!

Such a Pretty Sight!
Music

This delightful book is as engaging to sing about as it is to read! Make bear, bird, dog, and frog stick puppets to match the animals in the book. Then give each child one puppet. Lead youngsters in singing the song shown, instructing each child to hold her puppet in the air at the appropriate time. Then have the entire group hold up their puppets during the last line of the song.

(sung to the tune of "The Hokey-Pokey")

We see a brown bear there,
And a red bird in the air,
A small white barking dog,
And a slippery green frog.
The children think these animals
Are colorful and bright.
Oh what a pretty sight!

Ten Apples Up On Top!

Written by Dr. Seuss
Illustrated by Roy McKie

A lion, a dog, and a tiger have a balancing competition that leads to ten apples on top of each furry head.

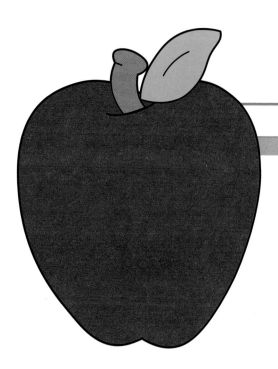

Balancing Act

Gross motor

In this classic Dr. Seuss book, all the animals compete with each other to balance a stack of apples on their heads. With this fun idea, your youngsters can test their balancing abilities just as the animals in the story do. Have students sit in a circle. Invite one child to place an apple cutout on his head; then encourage him to walk across the circle as the remaining students pass a real apple around the circle. When the youngster reaches the opposite side of the circle, the child holding the real apple then becomes the child to balance the apple cutout. Continue in the same manner as time allows.

Apples on Top Headband

Art

When a student wears this unique headband, she will look as if she is balancing apples on top of her head as the animals in the story do! Give each child a tagboard strip programmed as shown. Instruct her to glue several tagboard apple cutouts, one above the other as shown, to the strip. Next, encourage her to count the apples in the stack. Then help her write her name and the number of apples in the appropriate spaces. Finally, size the strip to fit her head and secure it in place.

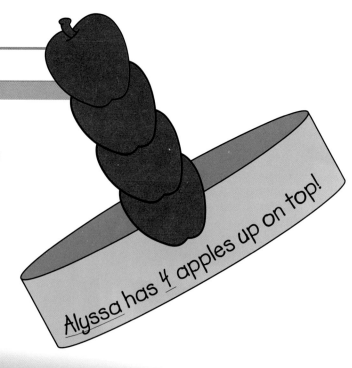

Alyssa has 4 apples up on top!

Stacking Apples
Literacy

Invite youngsters to help identify the rhyming words used in the story as the animals' apple-balancing competition continues. Position a large stuffed animal on the floor against a wall. Place a supply of apple cutouts nearby. Read aloud the story, emphasizing the rhyming words as you read. Encourage students to identify the rhyming pairs on each page. Each time a pair of rhyming words is correctly identified, invite a student to attach an apple to the wall above the stuffed animal's head. Finally, lead youngsters in counting aloud all the apples up on top!

Red Apples up on Top
Music

Here's a toe-tapping song that's just perfect for reinforcing this classic read-aloud. For extra fun, have youngsters name a different fruit and its color. Then repeat the song, substituting the words *red apples* with the new suggestion.

(sung to the tune of "He's Got the Whole World in His Hands")

I've got [red apples] up on top.
I've got [red apples] up on top.
There are so many, but I won't stop.
I've got [red apples] up on top.

The Apple Pie Tree

Written by Zoe Hall
Illustrated by Shari Halpern

Two sisters delight in observing the seasonal changes of their cherished apple tree. Colorful collage illustrations and simple text depict how the tree changes from winter to fall and provides the family with the best part of apple pie!

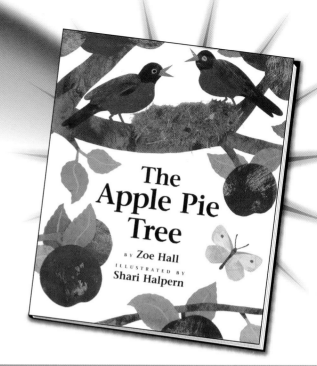

Apple Favorites

Writing

In the story, the apples from the apple tree become an apple pie. Youngsters are sure to be eager to try other types of food made from apples. Have students taste foods made from apples, such as baked apples, apple butter, and applesauce. Give each child a copy of page 105. Read aloud the prompt; then have him write or dictate for you to write a response in the space provided. Complete the title and help him write his name. When the pages are complete, bind them together between two covers with the title "Our Favorite Apple Treats."

Easy Apple Pie

Fine-Motor

The sisters enjoyed making and eating their own homemade apple pie. Your little ones will enjoy making and eating their own apple pie snack as well! Give each child two graham cracker halves and a disposable cup. Instruct her to crumble one graham cracker half in the bottom of the cup; then spoon one-third cup of apple pie filling on top of the crumbled graham cracker. Next, have her crumble the remaining graham cracker half over the filling. To complete this simple recipe, invite each child to spoon a dollop of whipped topping onto her cupful of apple pie. Mmm, good!

Crafty Apple Pie

Art

With this activity, students make an apple pie that smells good enough to eat—just like the one in the story! In advance, obtain a class supply of mini aluminum pie tins. Give each child a brown construction paper circle cut slightly larger than a tin. Invite him to cut white paper scraps and glue them to the circle so they resemble apple slices. Next, have him brush a thin layer of glue over the apples and then sprinkle cinnamon on the glue. Have him glue brown paper strips to the circle so it resembles a pie crust. Then encourage him to glue the circle to the top of a pie tin.

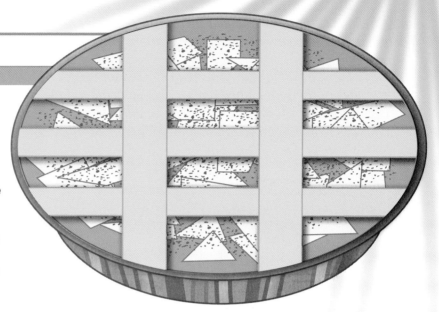

Seasonal Changes

Science

Invite youngsters to help make a display that shows the seasonal changes the beloved apple tree went through during the story. Attach a length of bulletin board paper to a table. Draw on the paper four bare trees; then write the name of a different season below each tree. Revisit the book and discuss with students the changes in the apple tree during each of the four seasons. Then provide youngsters with a variety of craft materials. Help students decorate each tree appropriately for the season, referring to the book as needed. Mount the completed project on a wall.

Winter   Spring   Summer   Fall

Nuts to You!

Written and illustrated by Lois Ehlert

Your youngsters will be nuts about this tale of a mischievous squirrel that will stop at nothing to get his food—including sneaking into an apartment through a tear in a window screen!

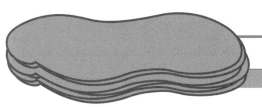

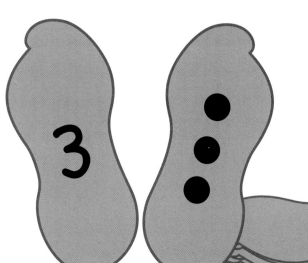

Nutty Numbers

Math

In this tale, a mischievous squirrel goes nutty over a handful of peanuts. Your youngsters will go nutty as well over this fun game of peanut matching! Program brown paper peanut cutouts with different numbers. Then program an equal number of peanut cutouts with dot sets to match the numbered cutouts. Place the separate sets facedown on the floor. Instruct a child to turn over one peanut from each group as you lead the remaining students in reciting the rhyme shown. If the number and the dot set match, she places the peanuts to the side. If not, she places the peanuts back in the piles facedown. Play continues in the same manner until all the peanuts have been matched.

Little squirrel, little squirrel,
Let's play a game.
Find two peanuts
That are the same!

Adorable Squirrel

Art

With this art project, little ones make an adorable squirrel—just like the squirrel in the story! Give each youngster a white construction paper copy of page 106. Instruct him to sponge-paint the squirrel with diluted black and brown tempera paint. Then have him spray the paper with a light mist of water. When the paper is dry, cut out the squirrel shape. Then have the child attach a hole reinforcer to the squirrel's head for an eye and glue a construction paper nose and construction paper whiskers in place. Finally, have him glue a nut cutout to the squirrel's paw.

Mischief Maker
Speaking

With this activity, students tell a story of animal antics reminiscent of that in the book. Attach a squirrel picture to a house cutout. Then program the cutout with the sentence starter shown. Read aloud the sentence starter and then hand the cutout to a child. Encourage her to think of what might happen if a squirrel snuck into her house; then invite her to finish the sentence. When she is done, instruct her to pass the cutout to a classmate. Continue in the same way until each child has had an opportunity to finish the sentence.

If a squirrel got into my house...

A Squirrelly Song
Music

Little ones will have a ball singing this song about the story. In advance, cut peanut shapes from brown craft foam. Invite a volunteer to pretend to be a squirrel. Then lead the remaining youngsters in singing the song shown, tossing the peanuts and having the youngster gather them when appropriate.

(sung to the tune of "Take Me Out to the Ballgame")

There's a squirrel up in my tree
Looking right down at me.
Sometimes he hides in the flowerpot,
Digging up all the bulbs he can spot.
So I threw the squirrel some peanuts,
And he took them away.
But I know that he will be back
For more nuts someday!

It's Pumpkin Time!

Written by Zoe Hall
Illustrated by Shari Halpern

Planting and tending a pumpkin patch keep a brother and sister busy from summer until Halloween. All their hard work pays off when they celebrate Halloween with home-grown jack-o'-lanterns!

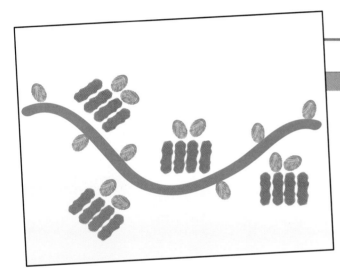

On the Vine

Art

The children in the story watch the pumpkins in their patch grow bigger and bigger on the vine. With this painting project, students make their own pumpkins on a vine. For each child, draw a curvy green vine on a sheet of white construction paper. Then have a child make a fist and press the top of her fist in orange paint. Next, help her press her fist near her vine so the print resembles a pumpkin. Repeat this process to make a few more pumpkins along the vine. To finish the picture, help each child use green paint to add thumbprint stems and leaves.

From Seed to Pumpkin

Music

Revisit the story with students to review the order of events. Then lead youngsters in singing the song below several times.

(sung to the tune of "Sing a Song of Sixpence")

Plant a little pumpkin seed;
Pat it in the ground.
Water and then watch green
Vines grow all around.
Soon there will be pumpkins—
The fattest we have seen!
We will carve the pumpkins
Right before it's Halloween!

A Variety of Vines
Math

Your little gardeners will be eager to tend to the vines in this activity, just as the siblings in the story tend to the vines in their pumpkin patch! Cut green yarn in different lengths to represent vines. Place the vines and a pair of gardening gloves in a basket at a center. A child dons the gloves and lays out the vines to examine their lengths. Then she orders the vines from shortest to longest. When she is satisfied with her work, she returns the vines and gloves to the basket to ready the center for the next visitor.

A Sequenced Story
Literacy

Youngsters review the sequence of events in the story by making these pumpkin-shaped booklets. Review the story with students. Then give each child a copy of page 107. Read the text and discuss the illustrations on each booklet page. Then help each child write his name on the cover and number the pages from 1 to 4. Help him cut out the pages and stack them in order beneath the cover. Finally, staple the pages together.

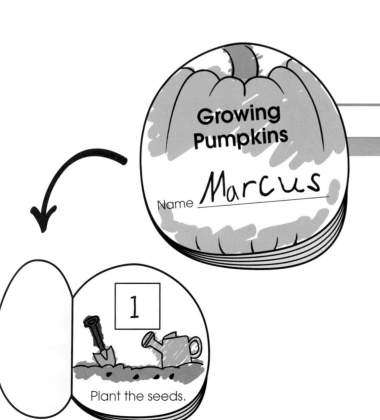

Red Leaf, Yellow Leaf

Written and illustrated by Lois Ehlert

This is the story of a sugar maple tree as told by the child who planted and adores it. The colorful collages on each page take the reader through the life of a sugar maple tree— from seed to beautiful tree!

The child picked out the tree at the garden center.

The Sugar Maple Tree

Literacy

In this simply written and beautifully illustrated story, a child plants a maple tree and watches it grow. Your students can help create a beautiful tree of their own with this story review idea. Mount to a wall a simple tree shape cut from brown poster board. After rereading the book, encourage each child to recall something from the story related to the maple tree. Prompt a student's memory with a picture from the story if needed. Write each child's response on a red or yellow die-cut leaf and invite her to attach it to the tree. Then use the information recorded on the leaves to review the story.

Colorful Leaves

Art

With this activity, youngsters make colorful leaves like the leaves in the story! In advance, fill separate spray bottles with slightly diluted red, yellow, or green tempera paint. Give each child a sheet of white construction paper. Lightly tape a maple leaf stencil on top of the paper. Then encourage him to spray-paint the paper. Finally, remove the stencil to reveal the artwork.

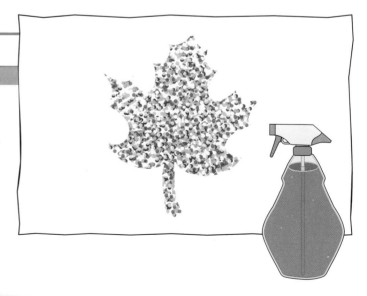

Red, Yellow, Red, Yellow
Math

Students are sure to enjoy this simple patterning activity that uses red and yellow leaves similar to the leaves in the story. Post on a wall a large brown paper tree limb. Provide a supply of red and yellow die-cut leaves. Attach several leaves to the limb in a simple *AB* pattern. Lead youngsters in reading the pattern aloud; then invite a child to choose a leaf to extend the pattern. After confirming her choice is correct, have her attach the leaf to the limb. Repeat the process with each remaining child. Finally, lead youngsters in reading the completed pattern aloud. If desired, remove the leaves from the limb and repeat the process using a different pattern.

Maple Tree Song
Music and movement

Youngsters will enjoy performing this action song about the tree in the story.

(sung to the tune of "My Bonnie Lies Over the Ocean")

A maple seed lies on the ground.	*Curl up in a ball.*
The seed grows to become a tree.	*Uncurl and kneel.*
Each year the tree grows a bit bigger.	*Stand.*
Until it is bigger than me.	*Point to self.*
Bigger, bigger,	*Hold arms like branches and sway.*
The tree grows much bigger than me, than me!	*Point to self.*
Bigger, bigger,	*Hold arms like branches and sway.*
The tree grows much bigger than me!	*Point to self.*

Go Away, Big Green Monster!

Written and illustrated by Ed Emberley

Yellow eyes, purple hair, and sharp white teeth sure sound scary! But not to worry! Thanks to the clever cutout pages of the book, this big green monster leaves just as quickly as it appears!

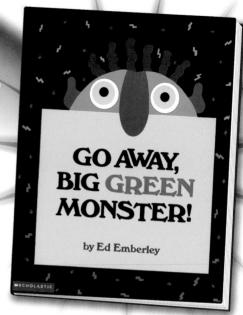

Color Paddles
Math

Youngsters recognize colors with this interactive rereading of the story. Make a class supply of construction paper color paddles that correspond to the monster's colors. Give one color paddle to each child. During a second read-aloud, instruct each child to hold his color paddle in the air each time the matching color is mentioned in the story. If desired, have youngsters exchange color paddles to get ready for another read-aloud of *Go Away, Big Green Monster!*

Big Green Monster
Art

With this simple idea, youngsters make their own big green monsters. Give each child a nine-inch green paper plate. Encourage her to cut or tear from paper scraps two yellow eyes, a bluish-greenish nose, a red mouth, white teeth, two bluish-greenish ears, and purple hair. Then have her glue the features to the plate to make a big green monster.

Monster Munch
Listening

Little ones are sure to enjoy making this yummy snack inspired by the monster in the story! Each child places a flavored rice cake on a plate. He spreads green-tinted vanilla yogurt on the rice cake. Then he places shredded carrots, mandarin oranges, a strawberry slice, and mini chocolate chips on the yogurt to make hair, eyes, a nose, ears, and a mouth. When his monster is complete, the child nibbles on his tasty creation!

The Monster Song
Music and movement

Youngsters can make the big green monster in this song disappear just as the monster did in the story! Have each child bring her green monster art project (see page 22) to your large-group area. Lead students in singing the song shown as they hold up their projects. During the final line of the sing-along, prompt students to whisk their monsters behind their backs. These monsters disappeared!

(sung to the tune of "Do Your Ears Hang Low?")

There's a big green monster
That has big yellow eyes.
It has sharp white teeth
And a big look of surprise!
But it won't scare me.
I'll say, "You get out of here!"
Then it'll disappear!

The Little Old Lady Who Was Not Afraid of Anything

Written by Linda Williams
Illustrated by Megan Lloyd

While walking home through the woods, a little old lady is confronted by a series of objects trying their best to scare her. When the objects show up on her doorstep, she helps them find an acceptable alternative to trying to scare little old ladies!

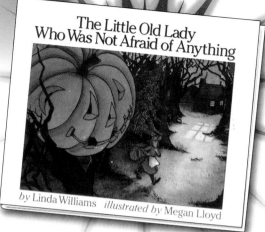

The Little Old Lady Who Was Not Afraid of Anything

by Linda Williams   illustrated by Megan Lloyd

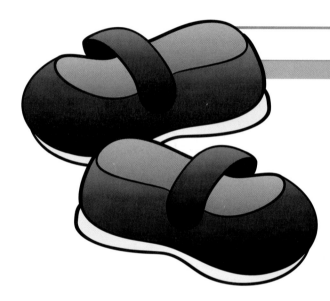

Clomp, Clomp!
Speaking

In this action-packed story, the little old lady was stopped in the middle of a path by two big shoes going *clomp, clomp.* Your little ones can share the sound their shoes make with this interactive rereading of the story. Invite each child to remove her shoes and place them on the floor in front of her. Next, read the story aloud, encouraging each child to pick up her shoes and tap them against the floor each time the shoes in the story go *clomp, clomp.* After the story, encourage youngsters to share other noises their shoes might make, using words such as *stomp, stamp, clatter, squeak, swish,* and *tap.*

Noisy Items
Literacy

Youngsters recall the sounds the objects make in the story with this flannelboard activity. Color and cut out a copy of the patterns on pages 108 and 109. Then ready the cutouts for flannelboard use. A youngster places the items on the flannelboard to form a scarecrow, using the book as a guide to place the items in story order and to recall the sounds they make. Those pants go *wiggle, wiggle!*

The Little Old Lady Who Was Not Afraid of Anything

Knock, Knock!
Art

What could be knocking at the little old lady's door? Have students recreate that scene with this art project. Give each child a copy of pages 108 and 109. Have him color each item on the page; then help him cut out the items. Instruct him to fold a 12" x 18" sheet of paper in half. Then encourage him to glue a circle to the front of the folded paper to make a doorknob. Have him unfold the paper and glue the cutouts to the right half. Then have him refold the paper. Encourage him to open the door and recite the noise each item makes in the story. Then prompt him to say, "You can't scare *me*!"

Helpful Scarecrow
Music and movement

Invite volunteers to act out the parts of the little old lady, the big shoes, the scary pumpkin, the scarecrow, and several crows as you lead the remaining children in singing the song shown.

(sung to the tune of "I've Been Working on the Railroad")

A sweet old lady left her cottage
And took a walk one night.
Soon she heard some big shoes clomping;
They were quite a sight!
Then she saw a scary pumpkin.
But on the very next day,
All these things made her a scarecrow
That shooed the crows away.
Shooed the crows away, shooed the crows away,
Shooed the crows away—caw, caw, caw, caw!
Shooed the crows away, shooed the crows away,
Shooed the crows away—caw, caw!

A Turkey for Thanksgiving

Written by Eve Bunting
Illustrated by Diane de Groat

Mrs. Moose tells Mr. Moose she wishes she had a real turkey for Thanksgiving dinner just like everyone else. So Mr. Moose goes out to search for a turkey. When he returns with Turkey, the guest is thankful that he is at the table and not on it!

Turkey Search

Literacy

In this Thanksgiving tale, Mr. Moose goes out to find a turkey to bring home for dinner. Your little ones also can search for a turkey with this sequencing activity! After reading the story, place in different locations in the room enlarged cutouts of the critters from page 110; then add details to a copy of the turkey cutout from page 111 and hide it from students' view. Lead youngsters on a turkey hunt, picking up each animal in the order it appears in the story. Then lead students to discover the hidden turkey.

A Dressed Turkey

Art

Turkey was not expecting to be the guest of honor at dinner, but luckily he was dressed for the occasion! With this cute craft, youngsters make a turkey similar to the one in the story. Give each child a brown construction paper copy of the turkey pattern on page 111. Instruct her to cut out the turkey and glue two fabric strips, as shown, to make its vest. Have her glue on construction paper scraps—cut to make a wattle, beak, and feet—and then colorful craft feathers to the back of the body. Finally, she uses a black marker to add eyes. Now this turkey is ready for dinner!

Dinner Food or Not?

Math

Mrs. Moose prepared a Thanksgiving dinner she was sure her guests would enjoy. Invite students to choose things their guests would enjoy for Thanksgiving dinner. Place an aluminum roasting pan in the center of your circle along with a grocery bag containing a variety of food and nonfood items (or pictures). Invite a child to pick an item from the bag and identify it as a food or a nonfood item. If it is a food item, have him place it in the roasting pan. If it is a nonfood item, have him place it next to the pan. Continue in the same manner with the remaining items.

Turkey's Special Seat

Music

Ask little ones how they think Turkey felt when Mr. Moose brought him to the Moose's house and why they think he felt that way. Next, ask youngsters how they think Turkey felt when he realized he was the guest of honor. Then lead students in singing this adorable song!

(sung to the tune of "Yankee Doodle")

Mr. Moose looked for a turkey
On Thanksgiving Day.
He met a lot of helpful friends
To join him on his way.
He found Turkey in a nest
And brought him home to eat.
Mrs. Moose invited him
To have a special seat!

I Know an Old Lady Who Swallowed a Pie

Written by Alison Jackson
Illustrated by Judith Byron Schachner

This little old lady looks sweet and harmless, but neither turkey nor cake is safe from her ravenous feeding frenzy! Youngsters are sure to chime in as you read aloud this delightful Thanksgiving Day tale.

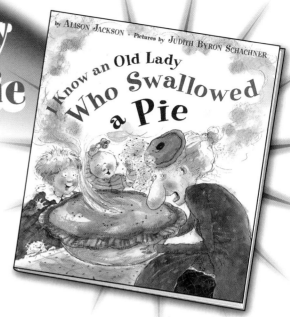

A Greedy Guest

Social Studies

In this hilarious holiday tale, a family is shocked by a little old lady's monstrous appetite and lack of mealtime manners! With this fun activity, your little ones will gain a better understanding of proper etiquette for sharing a meal. Cut out copies of the cards from page 112 so that each child has a card. Group youngsters with the same cards. Then don a hat, carry a purse, and introduce yourself as the little old lady. Lead a group retelling of the story, going to each group and pretending to ravenously gobble up each item as appropriate. Continue until all the food is gone; then lead a discussion about good manners and consideration for others when sharing food.

A Little Old Lady Balloon

Art

When the little old lady was finished inhaling Thanksgiving dinner, she became one of the balloons in a Thanksgiving Day parade. With this idea, youngsters make a little old lady balloon craft. Give each child a red construction paper balloon cutout that is slightly bigger than a large pie tin. Invite each child to decorate his balloon with green dots so it resembles the little old lady's dress. Staple the balloon to a pie tin, leaving a section open. Next, have the student add details to a construction paper head shape and attach the head to the top of the pie tin. Then give him a copy of the picture cards from page 112 to color and cut out. Finally, have him place the cards in the pie tin to take home and use for future story retellings.

A Whole Pie

Math

The Thanksgiving guest in this story wasn't satisfied with just one slice of pie—she gobbled down the whole pie instead! Show youngsters how the pie should have been shared. Decorate a light brown felt circle so it resembles a pie; then cut the circle into five pieces. Arrange the pieces on a flannelboard for students to view the pie as a whole. Then use the book's illustrations to count how many people should have had a slice of pie. Finally, invite a child to remove one piece of pie for each character as you lead the rest of the group in counting aloud. Then place the pieces back on the board to display the pie as a whole.

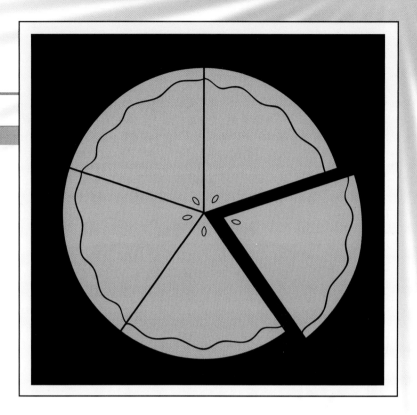

I Know a Lady

Music

Lead youngsters in singing this lively song to remind them of some of the foods the little old lady gobbled up during her holiday visit. Then encourage students to recall other things the little old lady ate that are not mentioned in the song.

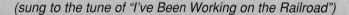

(sung to the tune of "I've Been Working on the Railroad")

I know a lady who, at Thanksgiving,
Swallowed a whole pie.
Then she had to drink some cider
Because the pie was so dry.
Next, she ate a roll and salad;
She ate a turkey too!
Finally, she ate some bread
And she grew and grew.

The Jacket I Wear in the Snow

Written by Shirley Neitzel
Illustrated by Nancy Winslow Parker

From her green jacket to her wrinkled socks, this bundled-up youngster is ready for the harsh winter weather. It's too bad all those itchy, bunchy layers are so uncomfortable! Captivate little ones with this rebus story full of repetitive text.

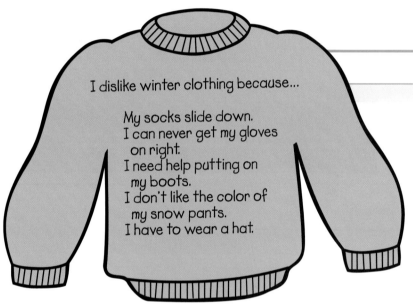

I dislike winter clothing because...

My socks slide down.
I can never get my gloves on right.
I need help putting on my boots.
I don't like the color of my snow pants.
I have to wear a hat.

Bundled Up
Literacy

The youngster in the story discovers that layers of bulky clothes are warm in the winter but are not always comfortable to wear. Have students share things they dislike about winter clothing with this activity. Post a large sweater-shaped cutout labeled with the sentence starter shown. Then ask youngsters to recall what the girl in the story disliked about her winter clothing. Next, have students share reasons they might dislike winter clothing. Then write their words on the sweater cutout.

Jazzy Jackets
Art

The little girl in the story has a warm yet plain jacket to wear in the snow. Little ones design their own fashionable snow jacket with this activity. Give each student a jacket cutout and access to a variety of art materials, such as cotton balls, pom-poms, sequins, rickrack, pipe cleaners, and paper scraps. Instruct each student to glue desired items to her jacket. Invite her to "model" her new snow jacket for the class.

The Jacket I Wear in the Snow

Winter Wear Removal

Literacy

The little girl in the book breathes a sigh of relief as each layer of winter wear comes off. Youngsters review the order in which the layers of clothes are removed with this idea. Gather winter clothing items similar to the ones the girl wore in the story and place them in a box. Revisit the story illustrations, drawing students' attention to the order in which the little girl's mother removes the girl's winter wear. After examining each illustration, invite a student to remove the corresponding clothing item from the box and place it in a row showing the correct order.

The Trouble With Mittens

Fine motor

Many things are more difficult for the little girl because of the winter clothes she is wearing. Little ones see how mittens make even simple things more challenging with this activity. Have each youngster bring a pair of mittens to school. Invite each child to don his mittens. Then give him a handful of packing peanuts and a cup. Prompt each child to pick up the packing peanuts one at a time and place each one in the cup. Then have him repeat the process without the mittens. Ask students to share whether the task was easier with or without the mittens and prompt them to give supporting reasons.

The Mitten

Adapted and illustrated by Jan Brett

Nicki takes his new snow-white mittens with him outside. After he unknowingly drops one of them, several critters find shelter in it. The border illustrations throughout the delightful tale provide clues to the story as it unfolds.

Will It Fit?

Speaking

Nicki's mitten stretches to hold several animals that crawl into it. With this activity, youngsters share predictions about what can really fit inside a mitten. Gather an adult-size mitten and a variety of large and small objects. Pass the mitten around the circle. While a student is holding the mitten, have him name one of the objects that he thinks will fit in the mitten and one that he believes will not fit in the mitten. Then have him test his prediction by trying to place the objects in the mitten. Continue until each child has had a turn.

Who's in the Mitten?

Art

The animals think the inside of a mitten is a perfect place to stay warm. With this fun idea, little ones find themselves inside a mitten as well! Give each student two mitten cutouts with holes punched along the edges as shown. Have each child use yarn to lace her two mitten cutouts together. Then have her decorate the outside of the project with a variety of craft materials. Next, have her place a photograph of herself in the completed mitten. Aah—nice and warm!

All Stretched Out

Math

At the end of the story, one of Nicki's mittens is much larger than the other. Little ones order and compare mittens of different sizes with this activity. Color and cut out a copy of the mitten patterns from page 113. Display them in random order on a board. Invite youngsters to help you arrange the mittens from smallest to largest. Then guide the students to compare the mittens using words such as *smaller, larger, smallest,* and *largest.*

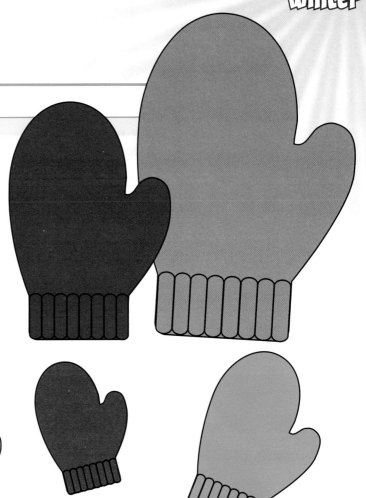

A Mitten Home

Music

Lead students in singing the song below to help them remember the story.

(sung to the tune of "Twinkle, Twinkle, Little Star")

A white mitten in the snow
Makes a home when cold winds blow.
Rabbit, Mole, and others hide.
They keep warm and safe inside.
A white mitten in the snow
Makes a home when cold winds blow.

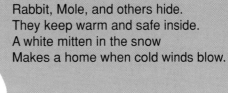

The Hat

Written and illustrated by Jan Brett

When a curious hedgehog gets a woolen stocking stuck on his spines, he becomes the laughingstock of all the other animals on the farm. But this clever little hedgehog convinces the animals that they all need similar headwear.

Stuck!

Music

Students are sure to love singing this little ditty, which revisits the beginning of the story. After leading your youngsters in singing the song several times, invite student volunteers to share what they would think if they saw a hedgehog wearing a sock on its head like Hedgie does.

(sung to the tune of "Yankee Doodle")

Some clothes were hanging on a line;
The wind began to blow.
Hedgie got stuck in a sock,
And he said, "Oh, my! No!"
Hedgie got stuck in a sock;
He said it's a hat.
Hedgie got stuck in a sock!
What do you think of that?

Dressed for the Weather

Writing

When the other animals make fun of him, the quick-thinking hedgehog shares the benefits of having a woolen sock stuck on his head. This encourages the other animals to find hats of their own. This writing activity invites students to share items they think would make good hats. Give each child a copy of page 114 and have her draw something on the hedgehog that she thinks would make a good hat. Then have her dictate her response to you as you write it in the blank. Invite each youngster to share her hat choice with the class and explain why she chose it.

The hedgehog's ___pot___ will keep it warm.

Sock Match
Math

In the story, Lisa hangs her laundry outdoors in the fresh air, including a pair of woolen socks. In advance, gather several pairs of socks and place them in a laundry basket at a center. Also place at the center a clothes drying rack. A child visits the center, removes the socks from the basket, and hangs matching pairs side by side on the rack.

A Prickly Pal
Art

Invite your youngsters to make a hedgehog—just like the one in the story! Give each child a light brown hedgehog cutout similar to the one shown. Have each child brush a mixture of glue and brown paint over a portion of the hedgehog. Then have him press pieces of spaghetti into the mixture. Finally, have each child glue a sock cutout to his hedgehog's head so it resembles a hat. As an alternative, have each youngster bring a sock from home, stuff it with tissue paper, and then staple it to the hedgehog's head to make the hat.

Bear Snores On

Written by Karma Wilson
Illustrated by Jane Chapman

While Bear takes his winter nap, forest animals take shelter in his nice warm cave. Their impromptu party eventually wakes Bear, but instead of being angry with his uninvited guests, he just wants to be included in the fun!

Bear eats a lot of food to get ready for winter.

Getting Ready for Winter
Science

This story begins *after* Bear has prepared for winter, with Bear sleeping cozily in his den. Remind students that real bears keep warm during the winter by having a sheltered place to sleep and a thick layer of fat on their bodies. Then lead youngsters in a discussion of what Bear might have done to get ready for his winter nap. Give each child a sheet of paper and have her draw a picture of Bear getting ready for his nap. Write a caption, similar to the one shown, at the bottom of each child's page and have her dictate a response for you to write in the blank. Stack the completed pages between two construction paper covers and bind the pages in a class book titled "Bear Gets Ready for Winter."

Popcorn and Tea
Art

The woodland friends nibble on popcorn in bear's den. Remind youngsters of this treat with a simple craft. Give each youngster a construction paper copy of page 115. Encourage her to color the tea black. Then have her use a pom-pom dipped in white paint to make prints on the plate (popcorn). What a tasty-looking wintertime snack!

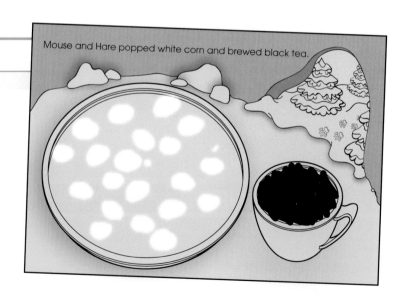

Mouse and Hare popped white corn and brewed black tea.

Party Animals

Literacy

Uninvited forest animals throw a party in Bear's cave while he is sleeping. This activity reminds youngsters of the animals present at the party! To prepare, color and cut out a copy of the animal cards on page 116 and ready them for flannel-board use. Make a simple cave cutout with brown and black felt. Place the cave on your flannel-board and place an animal inside the cave. Ask youngsters the question shown and lead them in the response, guiding them to say the appropriate animal name. Continue in this manner with each of the remaining animals. Save the bear for last, since he was the last one to join the party!

Teacher: "What's this critter doing in the cave?"
Students: "[Mouse] is having a party!"

Grumpy Bears

Gross motor

When Bear is first awakened from his nap, he is angry and grumpy. Eventually he cheers up and joins the party! Revisit the story with your little ones; then invite them to act like the bear. Have each child lie on the floor and pretend to be a bear in a deep sleep. Then make a noise with a party blower to awaken the sleeping bears. Invite youngsters to pretend to be angry to have been awakened. Guide them to snarl, roar, jump, stomp, growl, and grumble. Then invite them to dance around as if happy to be able to join the party. Repeat the activity several times.

Gingerbread Baby

Written and illustrated by Jan Brett

When Gingerbread Baby escapes from Matti's oven, he is chased around the countryside by a variety of people and animals. Meanwhile, Matti remains at home cooking up a way to catch this mischievous cookie.

oven   wall   barn   well   wagon   bridge   river   milk can   house

From Place to Place
Literacy

This activity enlists youngsters' help in recalling the places Gingerbread Baby visits as he avoids being captured. Draw an oven on one end of a length of bulletin board paper and glue a gingerbread house cutout (pattern on page 117) to the opposite end. To begin, attach a gingerbread baby cutout (patterns on page 118) to the oven with Sticky-Tac adhesive. Then revisit the story and invite youngsters to recall, in order, places Gingerbread Baby visits after leaving the house. As a child names each location, sketch it on the paper. Then encourage students to retell the story by moving Gingerbread Baby along the path until he is safely in his home.

Home, Sweet Home
Art

With this activity, students make a gingerbread house—just like Gingerbread Baby's! Give each youngster a brown construction paper house cutout (pattern on page 117) and a few cotton balls. Have each child stretch the cotton balls and glue them to the roof of the house so they resemble frosting. Invite each child to use a variety of craft supplies to decorate her house as desired. Then help her tape her house to another sheet of construction paper so it makes a flap like the gingerbread house in the story. Finally, have her color a copy of the gingerbread baby on page 118 and glue it behind the house.

Can't Catch Me!
Gross motor

Invite your little ones to maneuver through obstacles similar to the ones Gingerbread Baby faced in the story. In a traffic-free area of the room, arrange a row of blocks (wall), a large hoop (well), and a line of tape (bridge). Each youngster, in turn, steps over the wall, hops in and out of the well, and walks along the bridge. No doubt youngsters will ask to repeat the actions of Gingerbread Baby again and again.

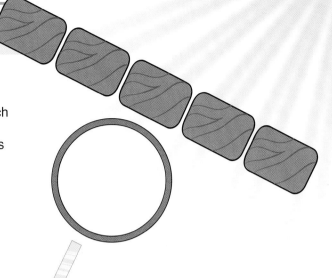

In, Out, and All Around
Math

With this activity, youngsters name positional words to show where the Gingerbread Baby is in relationship to his beloved gingerbread house. To begin, cut out a copy of the gingerbread house and one gingerbread baby pattern on pages 117 and 118 and ready each cutout for flannelboard use. Place the house on your flannelboard and place the gingerbread baby *beside* the house. Have students identify the baby's location. Then repeat the process with other positional words, such as *inside, outside, below,* or *on top of.*

The gingerbread baby is beside house.

The Snowy Day

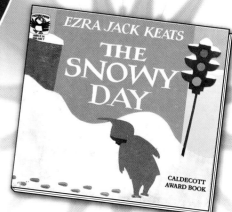

Written and illustrated by Ezra Jack Keats

Peter wakes up one morning to discover that snow has fallen overnight. He makes tracks in the snow and makes snowmen and snow angels. He even takes a snowball inside for later fun!

Frosty Footprints
Math

Peter has fun making footprints as his boots sink into the snow. Invite students to count similar footprints when they visit this math center. To prepare, place number cards in a decorative bag and put them near a length of white bulletin board paper and a supply of blue footprint cutouts. A child chooses a card and identifies the number. Then he places the corresponding number of footprints on the paper. If desired, he can turn the prints inward and then outward—just like Peter's footprints in the story.

A Snowy Song
Music

When Peter wakes up and sees the freshly fallen snow, he's excited to spend the day playing outside. Lead youngsters in singing the song below to review some of the activities Peter enjoys.

> *(sung to the tune of "If You're Happy and You Know It")*
>
> Peter saw the snow had fallen in the night. (Yay, snow!)
> Peter saw the snow had fallen in the night. (Yay, snow!)
> He made tracks and angels too
> In the snow so fresh and new!
> Peter saw the snow had fallen in the night. (Yay, snow!)

Fun in the Snow
Writing

In this classic tale, Peter finds many fun things to do in the snow. Ask each youngster what he likes to do in the snow and record his response on a sheet of light blue construction paper. Then encourage him to dot glue around his response and sprinkle glitter over the glue to make sparkling snowflakes on his paper.

Tomas

I like to build a snow fort with my brother when it's snowing.

Making Tracks
Art

In the story, Peter drags his feet and uses a stick to make lines and tracks in the snow. To make snow for your students to make tracks in, mix together equal parts of nonmentholated shaving cream and white glue. Place a dollop of snow on a sheet of dark-colored construction paper for each child and invite her to use a craft stick to make lines and tracks. Challenge little ones to write letters or numbers and draw shapes in the snow as well. When each child is satisfied with her project, set it aside to dry.

Snowballs

Written and illustrated by Lois Ehlert

On a perfect snowy day, a snow family is built using "good stuff": nuts, corn kernels, seeds, berries, a tie, and more! These snowpals visit for a while, but then the sun melts them away!

dad   baby   mom

cat   dog

Building Snowpals
Literacy

Each member of the snow family in the story is decorated with a variety of materials. Invite your little ones to create and decorate a snow family at this center. Label separate blank cards, each with a different one of the following words: *dad, mom, boy, girl, baby, cat,* and *dog.* Then prepare the cards for flannelboard use. Place the cards at a center along with a flannelboard, a supply of white felt circles in various sizes, felt scraps, ribbon, yarn, and other decorative items that can be used with the flannelboard. A youngster uses the circles and the other materials to make members of the snow family from the story. Then he places the corresponding card near each member of his snow family.

A Snowpal Snack
Listening

Some of the snowpals in the story are decked out in a tasty array of snacks. Invite students to make a snowpal with some similar tempting treats. Have each child spread whipped cream cheese on a rice cake. Then encourage her to add cereal pieces and sliced fruit to her rice cake to make a snowpal. When she's satisfied with the appearance of her snowpal, she eats her snack!

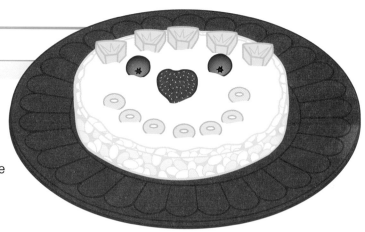

Personalized Pals

Art

Invite youngsters to create snowpals just like the ones in the story! Give each child three coffee filters and set out a variety of decorating materials, such as fabric, ribbon, yarn, paper scraps, pom-poms, and sequins. Have each child glue her coffee filters to a sheet of dark blue construction paper to make a snowpal and encourage her to glue items to the filters as desired. Display the completed projects with the title "Unique Snowpals."

An Icy Experiment

Science

When the sun comes out and the weather gets warmer, the snow family melts! This activity gives youngsters a hands-on investigation of melting. Place several cups of crushed ice in a container. Have each child form a snowball from the crushed ice and place it on a plastic plate. Invite each little one to describe how the ice looks and feels. Then have her place her plate in a warm or sunny spot. Invite the youngster to predict what will happen to her snowball. Encourage students to check their snowballs often and describe the changes they see.

SNOWMEN AT NIGHT

Written by Caralyn Buehner
Illustrated by Mark Buehner

Why does a snowman begin to look droopy and bedraggled? Why, it's just been doing what all snowmen do at night! Among other activities, these frosty friends spend their nights sledding, skating, racing, and drinking ice-cold cocoa!

Real
A snowman can have a carrot nose.
A snowman melts if it gets too hot.
A snowman can wear a hat.
A snowman can have buttons.

Make-Believe
A snowman can drink cocoa. (Draw bottom circle.)
A snowman can ice-skate. (Draw middle circle.)
A snowman can make a snow angel. (Draw head.)
A snowman can play baseball. (Draw arms.)
A snowman can go sledding. (Draw hat.)
A snowman can throw a snowball. (Draw scarf.)
A snowman can yell, "Wahoo!" (Draw a face.)

Is It Real?

Literacy

Real snowmen don't take off at night for merry-making in the park like the snowmen in this story. Or do they? Invite your youngsters to decide if statements you share about snowpals are real or make-believe. Read the statements shown (vary between reading real and make-believe statements), and have students determine whether each statement is real or make-believe and share why they think so. If the statement is make-believe, draw the suggested snowpal part on a large sheet of paper. After reading all the statements, youngsters will see a completed snowpal on the paper!

Cocoa Ice Pops

Science

Invite little ones to make their own version of the ice-cold cocoa the snowmen sip in the park. Give each child a personalized foam cup half-filled with warm cocoa and have him examine the mixture. Then invite little ones to predict what will happen to the cocoa if you put it in the freezer. After each student has shared his prediction, cover each cup with a piece of foil and have him poke a craft stick through the foil into the liquid. Place the cups in the freezer. After several hours, have students examine the frozen cocoa. Then have each child peel the cup away and enjoy his ice pop.

Hot COCOA

Wintertime Fun

Math

The snowmen in this story participate in several wintertime activities. Revisit the story and discuss with students the different winter activities the snowmen engage in. Draw a six-column chart on a sheet of bulletin board paper. Color and cut out a copy of the cards on page 119 and attach them to a floor graph. Help each child write her name on a snowball cutout. Then invite each youngster to announce her favorite activity as you help her place her snowball in the corresponding column. Finally, prompt youngsters to discuss the graph results.

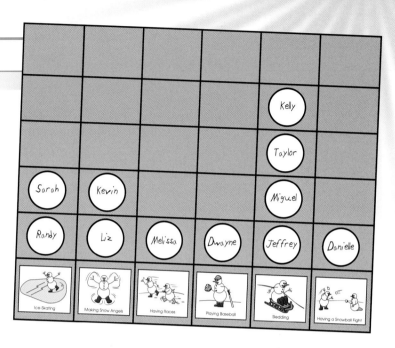

				Kelly	
				Taylor	
Sarah	Kevin			Miguel	
Randy	Liz	Melissa	Dwayne	Jeffrey	Danielle
Ice-Skating	Making Snow Angels	Having Races	Playing Baseball	Sledding	Having a Snowball Fight

A Snowy Night

Art

Invite little ones to create a snowy scene of snowmen at night. Invite each child to use a white crayon to draw snowy ground and snowmen on a black sheet of construction paper. Next, have him add any desired details to the snowmen. Then encourage him to brush glue over the drawing. Have him place his project in a tub partially filled with a mixture of glitter and salt. Have him sprinkle the mixture onto his drawing and then shake the excess back into the tub. Finally, have him add silver star stickers to his picture.

Hanukkah Lights, Hanukkah Nights

Written by Leslie Kimmelman
Illustrated by John Himmelman

This simple book offers an introduction to the traditions and symbols of Hanukkah based on one family's celebrations. Family love and togetherness are emphasized through the text and illustrations.

Hanukkah Traditions

Music

The family in the story participates in many Hanukkah traditions. Sing this song with your little ones to review some of these traditions.

(sung to the tune of "I've Been Working on the Railroad")

Hanukkah is such a nice time;
People celebrate.
Light the candles every evening,
Let's count them—there are eight.
Spin the dreidels and eat latkes,
Celebrate eight nights.
Hanukkah's a time for family,
The Festival of Lights!

Which Night?

Math

As each Hanukkah tradition is introduced, an ordinal number tells which night of Hanukkah it is. To practice ordinal numbers, show a random page from the story to students. Have students count the candles in the menorah in the lower right hand corner of the page (not including the shammash) to determine which night of Hanukkah is being described. Guide youngsters to convert the number of candles shown to an ordinal number. Turn to different pages to review other ordinal numbers in the same manner.

There are four candles. It is the fourth night of Hanukkah!

A Marvelous Menorah

Art

Youngsters make a colorful menorah—similar to the menorah in the story! Give each child a yellow construction paper copy of the menorah on page 120. Have her cut out her menorah and glue it to a sheet of construction paper. Then encourage her to glue a white strip of paper to the middle of the menorah so it resembles the shammash. Next, have her glue eight colorful candle cutouts to the menorah. Finally, have her squeeze a dot of glue above each candle and then sprinkle gold glitter over the glue so it resembles candle flames.

Luscious Latkes

Listening

The uncles in the story fry potato latkes, a traditional Hanukkah treat. Your little ones are sure to enjoy making and sampling some latkes of their own! Invite students to help you prepare the recipe shown. Bake the latkes as directed and allow them to cool before serving them to youngsters with sour cream and applesauce.

Potato Latkes
(Makes 20 small latkes)

4 c. refrigerated hash brown potatoes
1 egg, beaten
1 tsp. baking powder
½ tsp. salt
½ tsp. pepper
3 tbsp. all-purpose flour

Preheat oven to 400°. Line a baking sheet with aluminum foil and spray generously with cooking spray. Place the hash brown potatoes in a colander and press down firmly to remove excess moisture. Then transfer them to a large bowl and stir in the egg, baking powder, flour, salt, and pepper. Drop heaping tablespoons of the mixture onto the baking sheet and flatten them so they resemble pancakes. Bake for 20 minutes until the pancakes are light brown. Turn the pancakes and bake an additional 10–15 minutes until pancakes are golden and cooked through.

The Night Before Christmas

Written by Clement Moore
Illustrated by Jan Brett

In a snowy New England village on Christmas Eve, St. Nick and his eight tiny reindeer deliver gifts and toys to the sleeping children. The spirit of Christmas is beautifully captured in the brilliant illustrations that reflect this traditional poem.

Sleeping Students

Art

The children in this story are fast asleep and snug in their beds as St. Nick goes about his work. Invite your little ones to create art projects that show themselves tucked in bed, ready for St. Nick to visit them. To begin, photograph each student pretending to be asleep. Give each child a copy of page 121 and help her trim her photo and glue it to the bed. Next, have her glue a piece of fabric over her body so it resembles a blanket. Display the finished projects under the title "The Children Were Nestled All Snug in Their Beds..."

A Santa Song

Song

In the book's illustrations, two of Santa's elves stow away in his sleigh. Have youngsters sing this fun song about how his helpers are supposed to behave.

(sung to the tune of "Twinkle, Twinkle, Little Star")

Santa's elves load up the sleigh.
Soon it will be Christmas Day.
Sacks are stuffed with dolls and trains,
Ballet shoes and toy airplanes.
Santa's elves load up the sleigh.
Soon it will be Christmas Day.

Christmas Wishes

Literacy

As the children in the story sleep, "visions of sugar-plums danced in their heads." Revisit this page in the book with your students and guide them to understand that the children are dreaming of Christmas sweets they'll enjoy the following day. Then invite your little ones to share what they'll be dreaming of on Christmas Eve. Give each youngster a sheet of paper with a thought bubble as shown. Have him attach a photograph of himself under the bubble. Then have him draw in the bubble some things he would like to get for Christmas. (If desired, invite children to cut pictures of items from magazines and glue them on the page instead of drawing.) Bind the completed pages together in a class book titled "Our Christmas Dreams."

Cookies for Santa

Speaking

Guide youngsters to notice the drawings in the margins that show Santa's plate of cookies and then Santa enjoying one of the cookies. Then show youngsters an empty plate and explain that Santa's cookies are missing! Hold up a name card and recite the chant below, inserting the child's name and encouraging him to respond appropriately. After repeating the process with each name card, reveal a package of cookies and say, "No one stole Santa's cookies. They're right here!" Then give each youngster a cookie and place some on the plate for Santa as well.

Teacher: Who stole the cookies from Santa's plate?
Teacher: [Student's name] stole the cookies from Santa's plate.
Student: Who, me?
Teacher: Yes, you!
Students: Couldn't be!
Teacher: Then who?

The Polar Express

Written and illustrated by Chris Van Allsburg

Transported by a magical train ride to the North Pole, a boy is chosen by Santa to receive the gift his heart desires. He chooses a silver bell from a reindeer's harness. Once home again, the boy learns that the ringing of the treasured bell can only be heard by those who truly believe.

A Very Special Gift

Literacy

During your first reading of the story, stop reading after the sentence, "But the thing I wanted most for Christmas was not inside Santa's giant bag." Give each youngster a sheet of paper and ask her to draw on her paper what she thinks the boy wants most for Christmas. Invite each little one to share her drawing with the class. Then continue reading the story. Guide youngsters in a follow-up discussion of their predictions. Discuss with students whether any predictions were correct or whether anyone was surprised by the boy's choice.

Train Treats

Listening

Youngsters create a sweet version of the Polar Express train! Direct each child to spread frosting on a snack cake roll and press four chocolate sandwich cookies (wheels) and a caramel cup (smokestack) into the frosting as shown. After each child has assembled his train, invite him to indulge in his tasty treat!

The Polar Express
Winter

Frosty Windows
Art

The Polar Express travels through many snowy landscapes before it reaches the North Pole. Have little ones make their own frosty landscapes with this activity. To begin, add Epsom salts to a container of warm water, stirring the mixture until no more salt will dissolve. Then invite your little ones to imagine they are passengers on the Polar Express. Have each child use a white crayon to draw a snowy landscape on a sheet of black construction paper. Then encourage him to brush the Epsom salts mixture over his paper and allow it to dry overnight. The result is a landscape as seen through a frost-covered train window!

How Many Bells?
Math

The magical sound of a ringing silver bell is central to this enchanting tale. Obtain a desired number of jumbo jingle bells and place them in a transparent container with a lid. Ask each child to carefully examine the jar and estimate the number of bells inside. List each child's guess on the board. Then empty the jar and lead students in counting the number of bells out loud. Revisit students' estimates and discuss whose estimate was closest to the actual amount.

Kente Colors

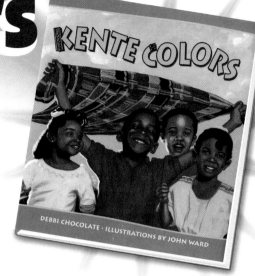

Written by Debbi Chocolate
Illustrated by John Ward

The simple rhythmic text and colorful illustrations in this book provide the reader with an enlightening introduction to traditional West African kente cloth.

Kente Quilt

Social Studies

The verse in this unique book explains the different meanings of kente colors and patterns. Review these meanings with your youngsters. Provide a supply of colorful paper strips that match the kente colors in the story. Invite each child to glue the strips to a construction paper square until a desired effect is achieved. Mount the finished squares on a large piece of bulletin board paper. Add a border and display the completed quilt on a wall.

Colorful Headwear

Art

With this activity, little ones make colorful headwear—just like the colorful headwear in the book! Give each youngster a wide black construction paper strip. Provide a supply of patterned scrapbook paper that represents the different kente colors. Have each child cut desired shapes from the scrapbook paper and then glue the shapes to her strip. When the glue is dry, size the strip to fit her head and secure the strip in place.

Kente Patterns
Math

Little ones are sure to have fun creating a colorful pattern reminiscent of the patterns in the book. Make equal sets of square cutouts in two of the colors shown in the book. Gather two squares in each color, and give each square to a different child. Place the remaining squares in a pile. Then position the students side by side with their squares to begin an *AB* pattern. Lead the group in saying the pattern; then invite a volunteer to name the pattern piece that would come next. After confirming his answer, have him remove the shape from the pile and then join his classmates to extend the pattern. Continue in the same manner with the remaining students.

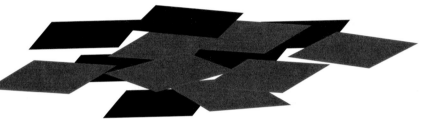

Colors So Bright!
Music

Invite volunteers to name different kente colors. After reviewing the symbolic meaning of each color, lead youngsters in singing the song shown.

(sung to the tune of "Are You Sleeping?")

Kente colors,
Kente colors
Are so bright.
What a sight!
There are red and darkest blue,
Green and yellow too.
Colors of
Joy and love.

Happy Birthday, Martin Luther King

Written by Jean Marzollo
Illustrated by J. Brian Pinkney

Celebrate the legacy of Martin Luther King Jr. with this book as it retraces the major events in Dr. King's life.

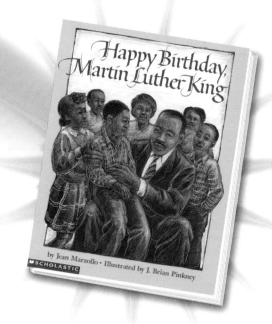

Happy Birthday,
Martin Luther
King Jr.!

All About Dr. King

Literacy

Youngsters tell what they learned from the book with this simple sharing idea. Mount a large birthday cake cutout on a wall. Ask a volunteer to tell something she learned about Martin Luther King Jr. from the story. Then have her attach a construction paper candle and flame to the cake. Continue in the same manner with other volunteers until the cake is covered with candles.

Celebrate in Harmony

Art

With this activity, youngsters make a project reminiscent of the celebration shown on the last page of the book. Give each youngster a white paper plate. Encourage him to draw a birthday cake in the center of the plate. If desired, help him write "Happy Birthday, Martin Luther King!" on the cake. Finally, instruct him to glue a colorful assortment of people cutouts around the edge of the plate as shown.

Peace Puzzle
Social studies

Enlist youngsters' help in thinking of ways to work and play together peacefully—just like Martin Luther King's dream in the book. Make a supersize heart cutout and label it "Happy Birthday, Dr. King!" Then puzzle-cut the heart. Invite a volunteer to name something she can do to work or play nicely with her classmates. If needed, prompt her with a situation along with solutions to choose from. Then give the child a puzzle piece and have her place it on the floor. Continue in the same way with each youngster, encouraging students to attach the pieces throughout the game to make a supersize heart.

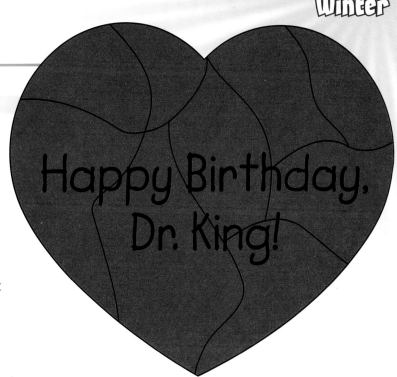

Happy Birthday, Dr. King!

Birthday Parade
Gross motor

Students learn from the story that people followed Martin Luther King's funeral procession in a "sad, loving parade." Help your little ones celebrate Dr. King's life with a happy, loving birthday parade. Give each child a party hat and invite him to choose an instrument. Lead youngsters in marching around your classroom or school, encouraging each child to play his instrument as you lead the class in singing a birthday song to Dr. King.

Substitute Groundhog

Written by Pat Miller
Illustrated by Kathi Ember

Poor Groundhog has the flu and is too sick to perform his once-a-year job of looking for his shadow. So he sets up interviews to find just the right animal to take his place on Groundhog Day.

Pop-Up Story Prop
Literacy

In the story, a line of animals wait to try out for the position of substitute groundhog. Your little ones will be able to name the characters and the order in which they appeared in the story with this simple story prop. Give each child a foam cup with a 2¼" slit cut in the bottom. Invite her to paint the outside of the cup brown. Next, encourage her to color and cut out a copy of a story strip on page 122. Help her attach the strip to a tagboard strip and then push the strip through the bottom of the cup. Finally, lead the group in a retelling of the story, encouraging youngsters to push each character up out of the groundhog's hole as it appears in the story.

Groundhog's Substitute
Science

Enlist students' help in identifying similarities and differences between the groundhog and armadillo in the story. Program two large sheets of paper with the headings shown. Revisit the story, directing youngsters' attention to pictures of both animals. Invite volunteers to name ways the groundhog and armadillo are alike and different; then record student responses on the appropriate Wanted poster.

> **Information Wanted**
> How are Groundhog and Armadillo the same?
>
> They can both see their shadows.
> They can both climb in a hole.
> They both like warm weather.

> **Information Wanted**
> How are Groundhog and Armadillo different?
>
> Groundhog has fur all over and Armadillo doesn't.
> Armadillo is from Texas and Groundhog isn't.
> Groundhog is sick and Armadillo is healthy.

Groundhog's Job
Gross Motor

Groundhog tries to teach each of his potential substitutes the important job they need to perform on the morning of February 2. Your little ones can try being substitute groundhogs as well with this fun action poem!

I'm a groundhog, fast asleep,	*Curl up on the floor.*
Snuggled in my hole so deep.	
I wake up on February 2.	*Stretch to awaken.*
And pop right up, that's what I do!	*Pretend to pop up from hole.*
I take a peek and look around.	*Put hand above brow and look around.*
Is my shadow on the ground?	*Shrug shoulders.*
If it is, winter's here to stay.	*Hug self and shiver.*
If it's not, spring's near! Hooray!	*Cheer.*

Groundhog's Flu
Music

Youngsters review the story with this fun song! Lead students in singing the song. Then ask little ones to identify the best substitute groundhog. It's Armadillo!

(sung to the tune of "If You're Happy and You Know It")

Oh, who could help the groundhog, who could help? (Was it mole?)
Oh, who could help the groundhog, who could help? (Was it eagle?)
Oh, who would be the best so that groundhog could get rest?
Oh, who could help the groundhog, who could help? (Was it bear?)

Guess How Much I Love You

Written by Sam McBratney
Illustrated by Anita Jeram

Little Nutbrown Hare loves Big Nutbrown Hare very much. As he describes his love in this enchanting tale, Little Nutbrown Hare discovers that he is loved even more.

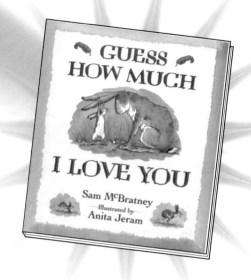

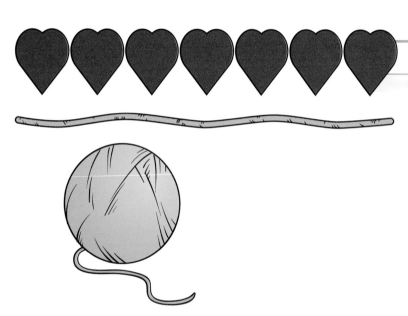

How Many Hearts?

Math

Little Nutbrown Hare stretches out his arms as wide as they will go to show Big Nutbrown Hare how much he loves him. Have little ones measure their arm span to see how much love they have. Make a supply of heart cutouts and place them at the math center. Have a child stretch his arms as wide as possible. Then cut a length of yarn the exact length of his arm span. Instruct him to lay his yarn on the table or the floor. Then have him place hearts side by side above the yarn. Ask him to count the number of hearts he used. Now that's a lot of love!

Lots of Love

Music

Little Nutbrown Hare learns something wonderful about how much Big Nutbrown Hare loves him. Lead little ones in singing the song below to review what Little Nutbrown Hare learns.

(sung to the tune of "Do Your Ears Hang Low?")

Little Nutbrown Hare
Stretched his arms into the air,
And he showed Big Hare
That he sure had love to share.
Big Hare's love was true,
And so what did Big Hare do?
He stretched his arms too!

Who Do You Love?
Writing

Little Nutbrown Hare finds many ways to tell Big Nutbrown Hare how much he loves him. Youngsters write about someone they love very much with this activity. Instruct each student to glue a flesh-colored circle cutout to a sheet of paper. Have her decorate the circle so it resembles a person whom she loves. Then have her write or dictate a sentence about how much she loves her chosen person.

I love my mom all the way across the ocean.

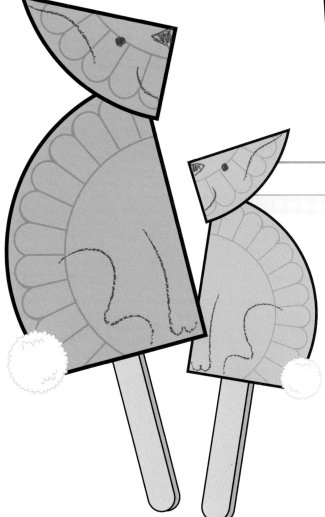

Plate Puppets
Art

Youngsters make big and little hare puppets to use when they retell this classic story. Have each student paint a small paper plate half and a large paper plate half with brown watercolor paint. When the plates are dry, help him trim them, as shown, to make a head and body for each hare. Then have him glue the heads to the bodies. Next, help him add details and a cotton ball tail to each hare. Then have him tape a jumbo craft stick to the hares to make stick puppets. Reread the story, encouraging youngsters to move each puppet when appropriate.

Roses Are Pink, Your Feet Really Stink

Written and illustrated by Diane deGroat

Gilbert is writing valentine poems to his classmates, but he can't think of anything nice to write about Lewis and Margaret. He writes mean poems instead, and isn't prepared for his classmates' reactions when they find out he's the author.

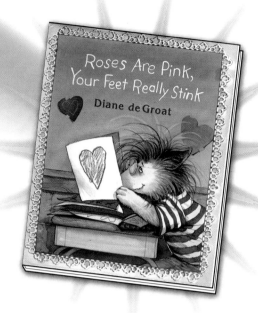

Valentines for Friends

Writing

Gilbert makes a particularly nice valentine for his friend Patty. In this activity, each youngster will make a nice valentine for a friend. Place student name slips in a bag. Have each student remove a slip from the bag. Instruct her to glue the friend's name slip to the front of a construction paper card. Then have her use craft items to decorate the front of the card. On the inside of the card, encourage her to write or dictate a nice valentine message and sign her name. Then collect and distribute the cards.

Heart-Shaped Cookies

Art

Have little ones make a heart craft reminiscent of the cookies Gilbert's mother makes for Valentine's Day. For the frosting, add a few drops of red food coloring to a bowl of glue. Then add sugar to the tinted glue and stir the mixture until it is the consistency of heavy syrup. Have each child attach a manila heart cutout to a slightly larger brown heart cutout. Have him drip two to three spoonfuls of the frosting mixture on the project and spread it around with the back of the spoon.

Roses Are Pink, Your Feet Really Stink
Winter

Missing Valentines
Math

Margaret and Lewis take a second look at their valentines and discover they have two from each other but none from Gilbert. With this activity, little ones use visual memory skills to figure out which classmates' valentines are missing. Glue a photograph of each student on a separate heart-shaped valentine. Place the valentines in a pocket chart. Invite youngsters to look at the chart, and then ask them to close their eyes. While their eyes are closed, remove two or three valentines. Have students open their eyes and examine the remaining valentines. Ask volunteers to name the missing valentines. Once the correct answers are revealed, return the valentines to the chart. Continue to play as described for several more rounds.

Apples are red.

Jeans are blue.

You share the blocks,

And I like you!

Strawberries are red.

Water is blue.

You look pretty,

And I like you!

A Perfect Poem
Writing

Gilbert learns his lesson in this story: It's best to write *nice* poems on Valentine's Day! Encourage youngsters to help write a Valentine's Day poem. Program a few sheets of chart paper with the poem starter shown. Then help youngsters supply words to complete a poem as you write their words in the spaces. Post the completed poem on a wall. Continue in the same way to create several nice poems that any classmate would appreciate!

Big Red Barn

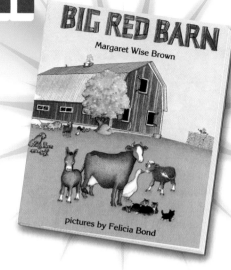

Written by Margaret Wise Brown
Illustrated by Felicia Bond

Visit the big red barn in the great green field to meet farm animals of every shape and size. From the tiny squeaking mice to the large lowing cows, this classic tale is filled to the brim with the wonders of life on the farm.

Moo

Neigh

Cluck

Woof

Oink

Where's My Baby?
Science

Many different adult and baby animals live in the big red barn. With this idea, youngsters focus on the sense of hearing while they pretend to be parent and baby animals. Discuss the sounds made by the farm animals in the story. Divide the class into two groups (adult animals and corresponding baby animals). Have each baby practice her individual sound. Then have all the babies make their sounds simultaneously. Encourage one adult animal to walk among the babies. When she finds her baby, have the pair sit in a designated area. Continue until each adult is paired with a baby.

In the Barn
Math

With this activity, youngsters help farm animals return to the barn to go to sleep—just as the animals do in the story. Place on the floor a large barn cutout, a variety of plastic farm animals, and other plastic animals that do not belong on a farm. Show the class an animal. Have a student place the animal in the barn if it lives on a farm or outside the barn if it does not live on a farm. Continue as described with the remainder of the animals.

Farm Favorites

Math

Have youngsters graph their favorite farm animals from the story. First, encourage youngsters to recall the animals in the story. Then place on a floor graph a card for each animal, as shown. Title the graph "Favorite Farm Animals." Invite each student to place a personalized sticky note in the column that represents his favorite farm animal. Then guide students in counting the number of notes in each column and comparing the columns.

Favorite Farm Animals

	Olivia			Michael
	McKenzie			
	Hannah	Cody	Sydney	Joey
Dakota	Tim	Charlie	Island	Jacob

All Around the Barn

Art

Students use their favorite animals to create a farm scene just like the one in the story. Give each youngster a barn cutout with the door flaps cut as shown. Have her glue the barn to a sheet of construction paper, leaving the doors open. Then instruct her to sponge-paint a grassy field around her barn. When the paint is dry, have her glue thin strips of yellow paper in the field to make a haystack. Finally, invite her to add favorite farm animals and other details to her scene.

We're Going on a Bear Hunt

Retold by Michael Rosen
Illustrated by Helen Oxenbury

Invite youngsters to come along on this exciting quest through wavy grass, a deep river, oozy mud, and more in this version of the traditional children's chant.

Dandy Descriptions
Literacy

Each obstacle the family encounters on its bear hunt is described with a pair of adjectives, such as "deep, cold." After the first reading of the book, cover the description of each obstacle with a sticky note. Guide students to create new descriptions of each obstacle. Then write the phrase on the appropriate sticky note. For example, change the phrase "long, wavy grass" to "green itchy grass." Once each obstacle has a new description, reread the story aloud to students. Then invite students to share which version of the story they like better.

Moving Along
Gross Motor

After reading the story, students will want to go on a bear hunt too. Color and cut apart a copy of the location cards on page 123. Review each location in the book along with the text that describes the family's movements. Tell youngsters to stand in an area where they have plenty of room to move. After you read the first card and show it to students, have the students say the appropriate text and perform the corresponding action. Continue the activity as described with the remaining cards.

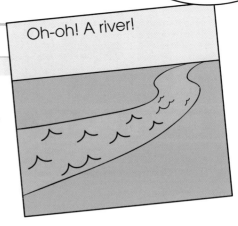

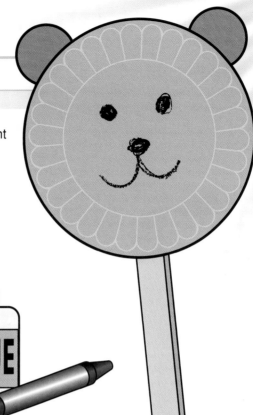

Over and Under

Math

This story provides the perfect opportunity to practice the concepts of *over* and *under*. Have each student make a simple bear puppet from a paper plate as shown. Prompt each student to hold his bear over an object, such as his desk. Then prompt him to hold his bear under an object, such as his chair. Give several more prompts using *over* and *under* to help students practice the skill.

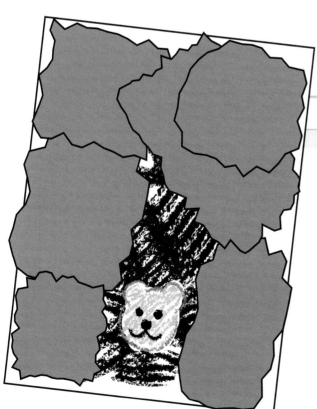

Bear's Cave

Art

The cave students make in this activity has a bear in it just as the cave does in the story! Give each student a white sheet of construction paper. If desired, program the paper with the outline of a cave. Instruct each student to tear a brown paper lunch bag into pieces and glue the pieces to her paper to create a cave. Then have her draw a bear in the cave opening. Finally, encourage her to color around the bear with a black crayon to make the cave look gloomy like the one in the story.

Growing Vegetable Soup

Written and illustrated by Lois Ehlert

A child and father lead youngsters through the steps of making vegetable soup from planting all the way to cooking! To enhance the story, labels accompany the bright simple illustrations.

From Seeds to Soup

Literacy

For this story-sequencing idea, share the following props with students: a vegetable seed packet, a small watering can, plastic vegetables, a large soup pot, and a plastic bowl and spoon. Invite students to discuss how each prop relates to the story. With students' help, order the props to show the sequence of events.

Peas, Please!

Science

Review the growth of the pea plant in the story—from a tiny seed to a vine with full-grown pea pods. Give each student a four-page accordion-folded book titled "Peas, Please!" To begin, have her color soil at the bottom of each page. Then encourage her to complete the following directions to make a book.

Page 1: Dip an unused pencil eraser in green paint and make a print on the paper (seed).

Page 2: Repeat the direction for page one. Then draw a sun and a cloud with drops of rain.

Page 3: Draw a small pea plant.

Page 4: Draw a vine growing in the dirt. Glue a craft foam pea pod to the vine. Use the process described under "Page 1" to make prints next to the pod.

Growing Vegetable Soup
Spring

Making Soup
Art

Your little ones make a yummy-looking pot of soup just like the one in the story. Have each child glue a green circle cutout to a sheet of construction paper as shown. Then instruct him to glue a smaller orange circle and green handle cutouts to the green circle. Have him cut paper into small pieces so they resemble chopped vegetables and then glue the vegetables in and around the soup pot.

Samantha

I put green beans in the soup.

Soup's On!
Writing

Lois Ehlert gives readers a recipe for vegetable soup at the end of the book. In the box below is a modified recipe just perfect to use with your classroom of little ones. Invite each student to add an ingredient to the soup pot. While the soup is cooking, give each student a sheet of paper. Instruct her to draw herself helping to make the soup. Then have her dictate or write a sentence to match her picture. Bind the completed pages to make a class book. When the soup is cool enough, give each student a bowl of soup and some crackers.

Vegetable Soup
½ packet onion soup mix
1 beef bouillon cube
5 c. water
1 small can tomato sauce
Fresh, frozen, or canned vegetables of your choice
Put all the ingredients into a large soup pot. Bring the mixture to a boil. Reduce the heat and simmer the soup for 30 minutes.

Tops & Bottoms

Adapted and illustrated by Janet Stevens

While Bear lazes on his porch, Hare makes a business deal with him: Hare will do all the gardening while bear sleeps; then they'll divide the crops equally. What's the catch? Hare tricks Bear into taking the least useful parts of the crops!

While Bear Sleeps
Music

Hare takes the best parts of the vegetables. Help little ones think like Hare with this activity. Gather a variety of vegetables, such as those mentioned in the story. Hold up a vegetable. Then lead youngsters in singing the song shown. Help youngsters decide whether the vegetable in question is a top or a bottom.

(sung to the tune of "Are You Sleeping?")

Top or bottom?
Top or bottom?
Can you tell?
Can you tell?
Is it top or bottom?
Is it top or bottom?
Can you tell?
Can you tell?

Growing Tops and Bottoms
Science

Youngsters can grow vegetables just like Hare! Help youngsters pour soil into a pot. Then encourage them to bury carrot seeds in the soil according to the directions on the seed package. Help youngsters water the seeds and then place the pot in a sunny location. As the carrots grow, have youngsters notice the tops of the vegetables. Then have youngsters watch carefully as you pull a carrot to reveal the tasty bottom of the vegetable.

CARROTS

Munch, Munch, Munch

Writing

The Hare family loves to eat vegetables. Give young-sters the opportunity to try some healthy vegetables too. Prepare for each student a plate containing vegetables of your choice and a small amount of dip. Help youngsters identify the vegetables and decide if each one is a top or a bottom. Encourage each child to nibble on his vegeta-bles. Then, on a sheet of paper, have him draw his favorite vegetable and write or dictate a sentence about it.

I like the carrots.
They are orange.

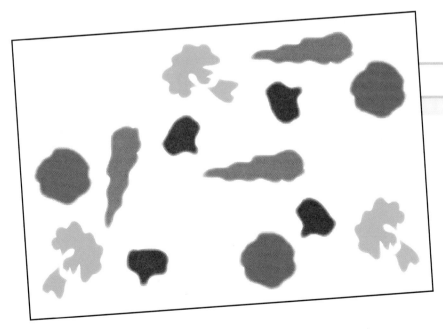

Vegetable Masterpieces

Art

Youngsters use the tops, bottoms, and middles of vegetables to create a vege-table masterpiece. Gather vegetables from the story, such as celery, radishes, broccoli, and corn on the cob. Slice the vegetables as desired. Then place each one next to a shallow container of paint. Encourage youngsters to press the vege-tables into the paint and then make prints on the paper.

The Grouchy Ladybug

Written and illustrated by Eric Carle

From sunrise and throughout the day, the grouchy ladybug challenges every animal it meets to fight. After a full day of badgering and bullying, the ladybug finally meets its match—the tail of a whale.

"Hey, you," said the grouchy ladybug.
"Want to fight?"
"If you insist," said the _bear_.
"Oh, you're not big enough," said the grouchy ladybug and flew off.

Ladybug Class Book
Literacy

Youngsters are sure to enjoy making this class book based on *The Grouchy Ladybug*. Duplicate a page for each student with the repeating lines from the story, leaving a space for an animal's name. Help a student name an animal that is bigger than the ladybug. Then write or have the student write the name of the animal in the space provided. Next, have her draw on the page a picture of the animal. Bind the pages together and read aloud the finished class book.

Ladybug Snacks
Math

To make this grouchy ladybug snack, a student spreads red-tinted cream cheese over a mini bagel half. She counts ten mini chocolate chips and then places them on the cream cheese. Then she tops the bagel half with a mini chocolate sandwich cookie (head) to finish her grouchy ladybug. Finally, she nibbles on her tasty snack.

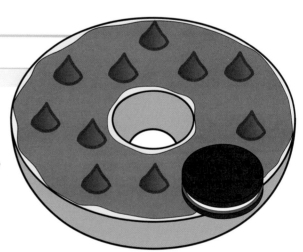

The Grouchy Ladybug

Ladybug's Lesson
Music

The simple song below summarizes the day the grouchy ladybug becomes a much nicer bug. Teach the song to students. Then invite students to create a fun movement to go along with each line of the song.

(sung to the tune of "If You're Happy and You Know It")

Oh, the grouchy ladybug said, "Want to fight?"
Oh, the grouchy ladybug said, "Want to fight?"
Then it met a quiet whale
That slapped it with its tail.
Now the bug's no longer grouchy; it is nice. That's right!

Grouchy or Friendly
Art

With this project, each student makes her favorite ladybug from the story. Have each child flatten half of a small paper plate. Then encourage her to glue torn pieces of red tissue paper to the plate. Help her trim any paper hanging over the edge of the plate half. Then instruct her to glue the plate half to a sheet of green construction paper. Next, encourage her to add black construction paper details to her ladybug. Finally, have her use a white crayon to draw a face on the ladybug to show whether she prefers the grouchy ladybug or the friendly ladybug.

Jump, Frog, Jump!

Written by Robert Kalan
Illustrated by Byron Barton

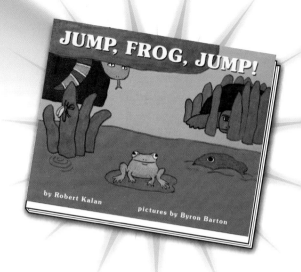

Follow a frog as it tries to catch a fly without being caught itself by fellow pond dwellers. Youngsters are sure to enjoy the predictable text in this cumulative tale.

Pond Sounds

Literacy

Youngsters bring this tale to life with an interactive rereading of the story. During this reading, pause briefly after each character is mentioned to have students supply the appropriate sound effects (see below).

> fly—buzz
> frog—ribbit
> fish—bubble, bubble
> snake—hiss
> turtle—splish, splash
> children—oh boy!

Jumping Frog

Art

Youngsters make their own jumping frogs with this fun activity. For each child, roll a sheet of green construction paper into a tube and tape it in place. Help each youngster cut four slits in the tube to make legs. Then have her fold the legs outward and trim the ends as shown. Encourage her to draw a mouth on the tube and then add eye cutouts and a curling ribbon tongue. Finally, help her attach a yarn handle to the project. She holds the handle and places the frog on the floor. Then she pulls up on the handle to make her frog jump. Jump, frog, jump!

Jump, Frog, Jump!
Spring

Hungry Critters
Music

The frog in the story jumps to safety on several occasions. Lead students in singing the song below to review the sly animals in pursuit of the frog.

(sung to the tune of the refrain from "Jingle Bells")

Jump, frog, jump; jump, frog, jump.
Jump up—do not stay!
Look—there is a great big [fish],
And you must get away!
Jump, frog, jump; jump, frog, jump.
Jump up—do not stay!
Look—there is a great big [fish],
And you must get away!

Continue with the following: *snake, turtle, net, kid, basket*

Jump, Jump, Jump
Math

The frog certainly does a lot of jumping in this story. No doubt your little ones will be eager to do some jumping of their own. Gather two large foam dice and have youngsters sit in a circle. Invite a child to toss the dice in the middle of the circle. Lead students in counting the dots aloud. Then say, "Jump, frogs, jump!" Have students stand and jump the corresponding number of times. Play several rounds of this fun math game.

In the Small, Small Pond

Written and illustrated by Denise Fleming

From the tall, tall grass leaps a bright green frog, who lands right in the middle of springtime in the small, small pond! Denise Fleming's vivid descriptions give readers a frog's-eye view of pond life throughout the year.

My Own Pond
Art

Many interesting critters live in and around the pond. Students make their own ponds filled with their favorite critters. Give each student an uncoated paper plate. Instruct her to color both sides of the rim of the plate using the side of a green crayon and the middle of the plate using the side of a blue crayon. Then have her color the area between the rim and the middle brown. Next, help her fringe-cut the rim of her plate so it resembles grass. Supply construction paper scraps and markers and invite her to add animals to her pond. Then help her fold the fringed portion of the plate so it stays vertical.

Wiggle and Waddle
Literacy

During this activity, little ones shiver, doze, and lunge just like the creatures in the story. Before beginning a second reading of the book, have students stand in a circle around an imaginary pond. As you read, guide youngsters to pantomime the movement described on each page.

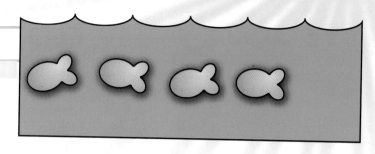
In the Small, Small Pond
Spring

Munching Minnows
Math

With this activity, little ones count minnows reminiscent of the minnows in the story. Give each student a pond cutout and several fish-shaped crackers (minnows). Announce a number and have each student count the corresponding number of minnows and place them on his pond. After checking each youngster's pond, have him remove the minnows. Then repeat the process with other numbers. Once the activity is complete, invite youngsters to munch on their minnows.

In the Pond
Music

Lead students in singing the song below to review some of the things the frog sees and does in the pond.

(sung to the tune of "The Farmer in the Dell")

The [tadpoles wiggle and jiggle].
The [tadpoles wiggle and jiggle].
They're in the small, small pond.
The [tadpoles wiggle and jiggle].

Continue with the following: *geese waddle and wade, dragonflies hover and shiver, turtles drowse and doze, herons lash and lunge, minnows splitter and splatter, whirligigs circle and swirl, swallows sweep and swoop, crayfish click and clack, geese dabble and dip, raccoons splish and splash, muskrats pile and pack*

Mrs. Wishy-Washy

Written by Joy Cowley
Illustrated by Elizabeth Fuller

When the farm animals roll in the mud, Mrs. Wishy-Washy gives them a good scrubbing in her washtub. What do the animals do when they're squeaky clean? Why, they jump back into the mud of course!

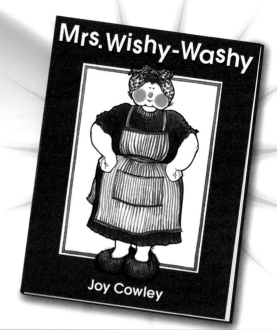

"Oh lovely mud," said <u>Lee</u>.
"I would <u>dance</u> in it."

Lovely Mud
Writing

The animals in the book jump, roll, and paddle in a mud puddle. Little ones express what they would like to do in a mud puddle with this activity. Program a strip of paper with the words shown. Next, have each child fingerpaint on a sheet of paper with brown paint. Then have her draw a picture or attach a trimmed photograph of herself to the resulting puddle. Have her write her name on the first blank of the strip. Then have her dictate as you write her word(s) in the appropriate space what she would do in the mud puddle.

Muddy Treat
Listening

The animals in the story love mud. Serve youngsters more muddy animals at snacktime. Mix a batch of instant chocolate pudding (mud). Give each student a disposable plate. Have each child scoop a small serving of pudding onto her plate. Then instruct her to put five animal-shaped crackers beside the mud. Encourage her to let the animals frolic in the mud before she eats them.

Mrs. Wishy-Washy
Spring

Bath Time

Math

The cow, duck, and pig in this activity get muddy just like the animals in the story. Give each child a copy of page 124. Have students practice counting to ten. Then encourage each student to press her finger on a brown ink pad and make ten fingerprints (muddy spots) on each animal. If desired, help each child cut out the patterns.

In the Tub

Art

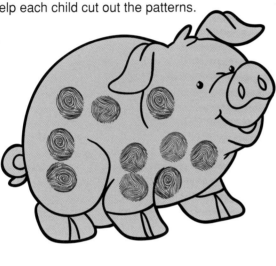

Each animal gets a bath in Mrs. Wishy-Washy's tub. Youngsters give an animal a bath in their own tub with this activity. Cut out copies of the animal patterns on page 124 so there is one animal per student. Instruct each child to color his animal so it resembles one of the dirty animals from the story. Then have him glue the animal to a sheet of construction paper. Encourage him to glue a washtub cutout to the paper so it partially covers the animal. Finally, invite him to dip the end of a marker cap in white paint and then press the cap on his paper to make bubbles.

One Duck Stuck

Written by Phyllis Root
Illustrated by Jane Chapman

Oh, no! A duck is stuck in the muck—yuck! Watch as a host of animals come to help the duck get unstuck—what luck! Filled with engaging language and silly sounds, this counting book is sure to please little ones!

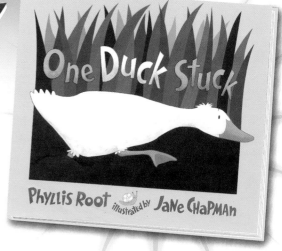

In the Muck

Art

Poor duck—it's stuck! Little ones make their own stuck ducks with this cute project. Give each student a sheet of green construction paper and two paper plate halves. Have her fringe-cut the top portion of her paper. Then have her glue one plate half to the paper to make the duck's body. Help her cut the center from the remaining plate half and glue it to the paper so it resembles the duck's head. Have her attach bill and leg cutouts to the project. Finally, encourage her to brush brown paint along the bottom of the paper to make the muck.

Hop, Slither, Slide

Gross motor

Here's a fun idea for an interactive rereading of the story! As you read aloud the story, have youngsters join in chanting "We can! We can!" each time different animals chant the words. Then as you read the next paragraph, prompt students to stand and move like the type of animal coming to the duck's aid.

Who Can Help?
Social studies

Youngsters can work together just like the animals in the story. Divide the class into groups of three students. Give each group a box of crayons. Instruct one student in each group to spill the crayons. Then have her recite the duck's lines from the story: "Help! Help! Who can help?" Have the rest of the group respond, "We can! We can!" and then help her pick up the crayons. Continue the activity until each child has had a turn to give and receive assistance.

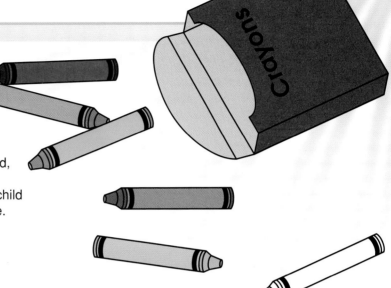

We Can Help!
Literacy

Give each student a sheet of paper and ask him to draw how he would help the duck get out of the muck. Invite him to share his drawing. Then bind the pages together and place them in your reading center.

The Very Hungry Caterpillar

Written and illustrated by Eric Carle

Join a ravenous caterpillar as he eats his way through the days of the week. By Saturday he has eaten so much he has a stomachache. Then he eats a leaf and builds a cocoon. After more than two weeks, he emerges as a beautiful butterfly.

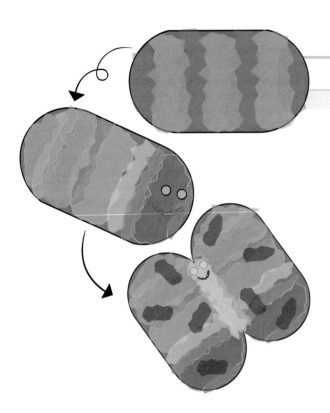

From Cocoon to Butterfly
Art

Here's an art project that will help little ones retell the story. For each child, cut an elongated oval from a folded sheet of brown construction paper, leaving the fold intact as shown. Have each child fold his project and glue brown and orange tissue paper strips to one side so that side resembles a cocoon. Then, with the project still folded, have him make a caterpillar by gluing colorful tissue paper strips and attaching sticky-dot eyes with green pupils to the project's other side. Next, encourage him to unfold the project and glue tissue paper pieces to the inside so it resembles a butterfly. Encourage youngsters to use the prop to retell the story.

Caterpillar's Fruit Salad
Literacy

During the week, the hungry caterpillar eats several kinds of fruit. Little ones review the order in which the fruits are eaten as well as make a tasty fruit salad with this activity. In advance, ask each student's family to send a can of fruit to school. Color and cut out copies of the fruit patterns on page 125. Punch a hole in each fruit cutout. Revisit the part of the story that recalls the caterpillar's fruit choices. Then display the fruit in random order in front of the students. Help students attach the fruit to your board in story order. Then have little ones make and eat their own fruit salad.

Lots of Caterpillars
Math

Little ones make oodles of very hungry caterpillars with this activity. Gather a class supply of large index cards and write a number at the top of each card. Give each student a card and access to an ink pad. Have him identify the number and then make the corresponding number of fingerprint caterpillars on his card.

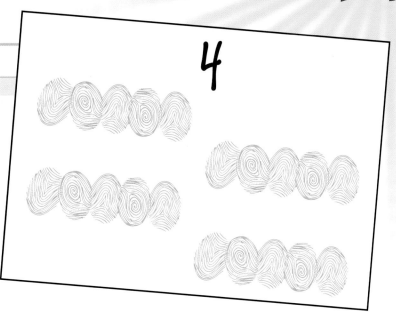

Becoming a Butterfly
Music

Lead little ones in singing the song below to review how the caterpillar transforms into a beautiful butterfly.

(sung to the tune of "The Itsy-Bitsy Spider")

A hungry caterpillar
Woke up in the warm sun.
He ate through an apple
Some pears, and then some plums.
He got fat and spun
A cocoon that kept him dry.
Then he nibbled his way out,
And he was a butterfly.

Waiting for Wings

Written and illustrated by Lois Ehlert

The vivid garden illustrations and rhyming text cheerfully teach little ones about the life cycle of a butterfly. Use this book and these activities to help youngsters spread their own creative wings.

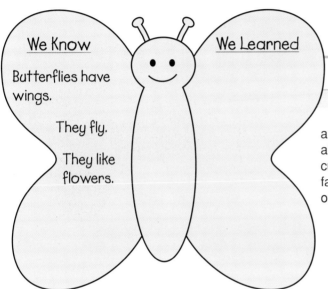

We Know

Butterflies have wings.

They fly.

They like flowers.

We Learned

Fluttery Facts
Literacy

For this prereading activity, post a large butterfly cutout on a wall. Invite students to share information they already know about butterflies. Write their responses on the left side of the cutout. Then read the book aloud. Have students share the facts they learned while listening to the story. List these facts on the right side of the cutout.

Song of the Butterfly
Music

Lead students in singing this song to review the events of the book.

(sung to the tune of "Do Your Ears Hang Low?")

Caterpillar spins
A hard case and stays inside.
It's a quiet place;
It's a place where it can hide.
As it hides, it turns
Into a pretty butterfly
And flies to the sky.

Butterfly Changes
Science

With this idea, little ones use simple props to order the events from the story. Give each student a small bag containing the following items: a small white pom-pom (egg), a short length of pipe cleaner (caterpillar), a shell-shaped pasta (chrysalis), and a butterfly cutout. Instruct her to remove the items from the bag. Explain what stage of the life cycle each item represents. Then have her order the items to show the life cycle of a butterfly. After checking her work, have her return the items to the bag.

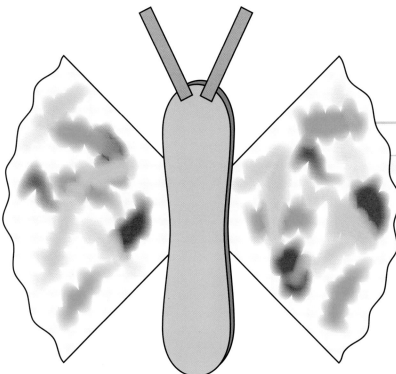

Bright Beauties
Art

Have youngsters make brightly colored butterflies similar to the ones in the story! Give each student a coffee filter half. Instruct him to use washable markers to make designs on one half of the filter. Then have him fold the filter in half and spray it with water until the colors begin to run. When the filter is dry, have him cut it along the fold and attach the two pieces to a painted wooden ice cream spoon. Finally, have him attach construction paper antennae to the spoon.

Green Eggs and Ham

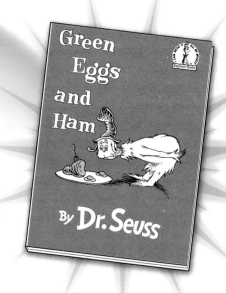

Written and illustrated by Dr. Seuss

Do you like green eggs and ham? Sam poses this question and goes through a series of outlandish scenarios in order to tempt the main character to try this colorful cuisine. When the character tries the eggs and ham, he is surprised to find out that he likes them.

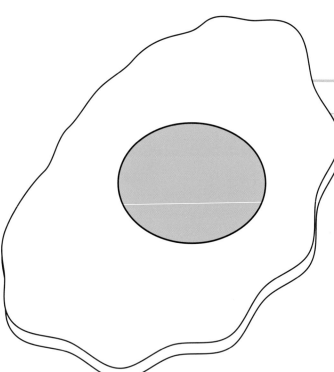

Egg, Leg, Beg...
Literacy

With this activity, little ones make rhymes just as Dr. Seuss does in this whimsical tale. Fashion from craft foam a simple fried egg cutout with a green yolk. Seat yourself in a circle with your students. Say the word *egg* and pass the egg to the youngster beside you. Have him take the egg and state a real or nonsense word that rhymes with *egg*. After he says his word, prompt him to pass the egg to the next student. Have this student state another rhyming word and then pass the egg. Continue in this manner until each student has had a turn.

Sam's Plate
Art

Little ones serve up a plate of green eggs and ham just like the one in the story. Invite each student to color a paper plate. Then instruct him to slightly stretch two cotton balls and glue them to his plate. Encourage him to glue a green yolk cutout to each cotton ball. Then have him glue a green ham shape beside the eggs.

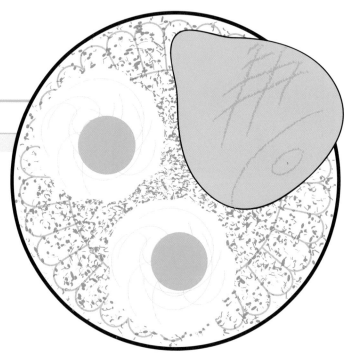

Are They Tasty?
Math

The character in the story is convinced he won't like green eggs and ham—perhaps because they are green. Give little ones a chance to try green eggs with this activity. Post a chart similar to the one shown. Then cook a batch of green-tinted scrambled eggs. Give each student a personalized sticky note along with a small amount of eggs to taste. After she tastes the eggs, invite her to place her sticky note on the appropriate side of the chart. Guide students in counting and comparing the chart results.

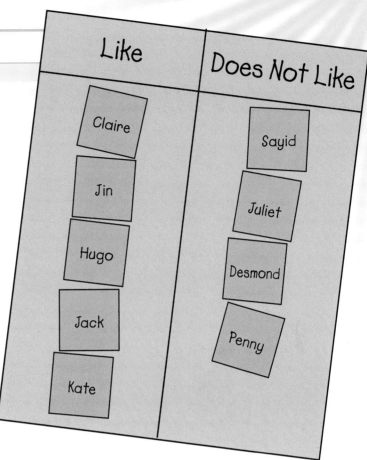

Like	Does Not Like
Claire	Sayid
Jin	Juliet
Hugo	Desmond
Jack	Penny
Kate	

Pass the Plate
Gross motor

Sam carries that plate of green eggs and ham everywhere! Little ones try carrying a plate like Sam's for this activity. Cut two eggs and a ham steak from craft foam and place them on a sturdy paper plate. Have students stand in a row side by side. Hand the first child the plate and encourage him to quickly pass it to the person next to him. Have youngsters continue to pass the plate down the row without dropping the eggs or the ham.

The Golden Egg Book

Written by Margaret Wise Brown

Illustrated by Leonard Weisgard

A little brown bunny wonders what is inside an egg. He tries to break the egg until he gets so tired he falls asleep. He awakens to find that his egg is gone and a duck is there instead. Now he has a new friend!

What's Inside?

Literacy

For this prereading activity, read aloud the first page of the story and then give each student an egg cutout. Instruct her to draw what she thinks is inside the egg. Ask her to share her guess. Then finish reading the story aloud to reveal what is really inside the egg.

Animals in Eggs

Art

The little bunny has many ideas about what could be inside his egg. In this activity a youngster gets to put his favorite animal inside an egg. Give each child a tissue paper egg cutout and a construction paper egg cutout. Have each student use fine-tip markers to make multicolored dots on the tissue paper. Then have him use a dark-colored crayon to draw an animal on the construction paper. Help him stack the eggs so the tissue paper is on top. Then staple the eggs together. The animal shows through the tissue paper!

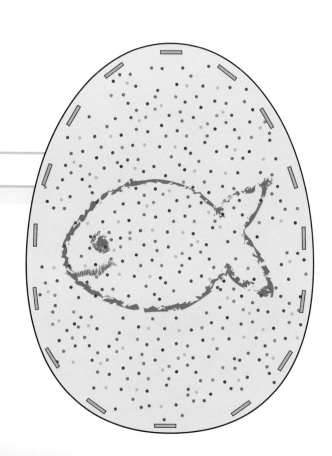

Egg Sort
Math

The little bunny's egg is blue, but eggs come in all sizes and colors. Gather a class supply of plastic eggs in various colors and sizes. Also gather several baskets. Help students sort the eggs into the baskets by color. Then ask youngsters whether there is a different way they can sort the eggs, guiding them to conclude that the eggs can be sorted by size. Remove the eggs from the baskets and help youngsters sort them back into the baskets by size.

Fabulous Floral Egg
Fine motor

With the help of your little ones, make a beautiful egg like the one on the cover of *The Golden Egg Book*. Attach a brightly colored ribbon to a large egg cutout. Then place the egg in your art center along with gardening catalogs, scissors, and glue. Youngsters cut pictures from the catalogs and attach them to the egg. After each youngster has had an opportunity to add to the egg, display it in your classroom.

One Hot Summer Day

Written and illustrated by Nina Crews

Experience a summer day in the city through the eyes of an energetic girl. She makes chalk drawings, teases her shadow, and eats grape ice pops all on a hot summer day.

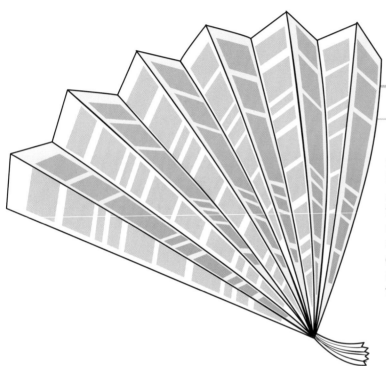

Summer Day Activities

Speaking

The little girl in the story finds oodles of fun things to do on a hot summer day. Find out what your little ones like to do on a hot day with this activity. Accordion-fold a newspaper page so it resembles the fan from the story. Give the fan to a child and encourage her to share what she likes to do on a hot summer day. When she is finished, give the fan to a different student. Repeat the process several times until all youngsters have had an opportunity to hold the fan and share their ideas.

Hot-Day Ditty

Music

Spotlight the events in the story with this song and these props. Have each youngster make a stick puppet with a sun on one side and raindrops on the opposite side, as shown. Lead students in singing the first verse of the song as they hold up their sun puppets. Then have youngsters flip their puppets to the raindrops as you lead them in singing the second verse.

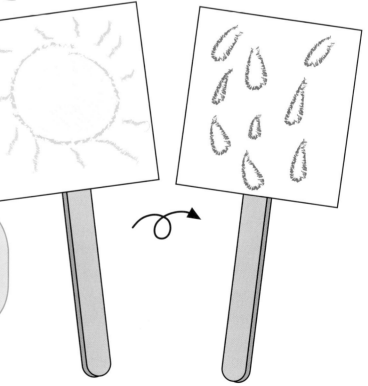

(sung to the tune of "Hot Cross Buns")

Hot, hot day.	Hot, hot day.
Hot, hot, day.	Hot, hot day.
It is much too hot to play.	Here comes rain; now I can play.
Hot, hot, day.	It's cooler. Hooray!

Sweet and Juicy
Art

With this activity, little ones make yummy-looking grape ice pops similar to the one the little girl eats in the story. In advance, use food coloring to tint gel glue purple. Have each child attach two craft sticks and a purple ice pop cutout to a sheet of construction paper as shown. Then have her use a paintbrush to dab the purple glue on the ice pop and to make several drips below it. Finally, instruct her to sprinkle purple glitter on the wet glue.

Staying Cool
Science

The little girl and others in the story use several methods to keep cool. With this display, youngsters share ways from the book to keep cool as well as some ideas of their own. Post a sun cutout without rays. Then cut several yellow construction paper rays as shown. Ask students to recall from the story ways the little girl and others keep cool. Write each idea on a separate ray and attach it to the sun. Once all the ways from the story are named, invite little ones to add their own keeping-cool ideas.

Jamberry

Written and illustrated by Bruce Degen

Follow a lovable bear and his boy companion through their adventures in an imaginary berry-filled land. Captivating rhymes and detailed illustrations are sure to leave youngsters hungry for repeated readings of this story!

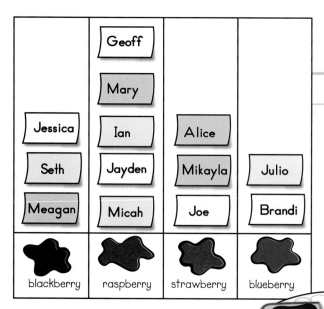

	Geoff		
	Mary		
Jessica	Ian	Alice	
Seth	Jayden	Mikayla	Julio
Meagan	Micah	Joe	Brandi
blackberry	raspberry	strawberry	blueberry

A "Berry" Good Graph
Math

In this classic tale, the bear and the boy encounter a variety of flavorful berries. Your youngsters will encounter flavorful berries as well in this simple graphing activity. Gather four different types of jam. Display a graph similar to the one shown. Have each child cut a slice of bread into four pieces and spread a different type of jam on each piece. After she nibbles on her bread, have her decide which jam is her favorite and then attach a personalized sticky note to the appropriate column on the graph. Finally, lead youngsters in counting and comparing the number of notes in each column.

Hat Full of Berries
Art

With this activity, youngsters make strawberry-filled hats—just like the boy's hat in the story! Give each youngster a construction paper copy of page 126 and have her color the hat yellow. Instruct her to press the tines of a fork in brown paint and then press the fork on the hat to make the crosshatched pattern of the hat in the story. Then have her make red thumbprints in and around the hat. When the paint is dry, encourage her to use fine-tip permanent markers to add details to the fingerprints so they resemble strawberries.

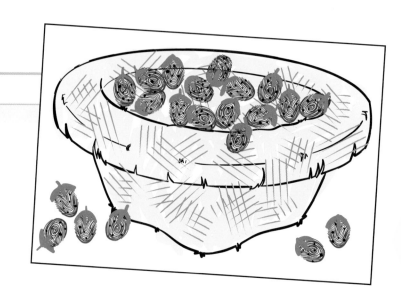

Real and Pretend

Literacy

Enlist youngsters' help in distinguishing between the real and imaginative berries named in the book. Gather two adult shoes and label one shoe *real* and the second shoe *pretend*. Write the names of the real and pretend berries from the story on separate cards. Revisit the story, reminding youngsters how the shoe in the book is filled with berries. Then show youngsters a card and name the berry. Ask, "Is this a real berry or a pretend berry?" After youngsters decide on a category for the berry, have a child place the card in the appropriate shoe.

blackberry
shoeberry
jamberry
blueberry
Pretend
Real
strawberry
raspberry
trackberry
starberry

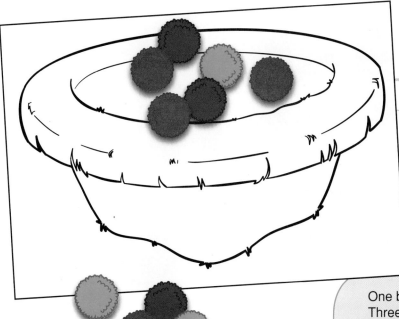

Count and Chant

Math

Students are sure to enjoy counting berries in this adorable rhyme reminiscent of the text of *Jamberry*. Give each youngster ten pom-poms (berries) and a copy of the hat picture on page 126. Have each child place his berries next to the hat. Next, lead students in reciting the rhyme shown, having each child place a berry on the hat for each number named.

One berry, two berry, too good to be true berry,
Three berry, four berry, please give us some more berry.
Five berry, six berry, won't you pick them quick berry?
Seven berry, eight berry, put them on a plate berry.
Nine berry, ten berry, say the rhyme again berry.

The Little Mouse, The Red Ripe Strawberry, and THE BIG HUNGRY BEAR

Written by Don and Audrey Wood
Illustrated by Don Wood

Little ones will delight in this sweet story as a mouse tries one thing after another to save its delicious strawberry from a big hungry bear. In the end, the mouse is tricked into sharing its strawberry with the narrator.

How old are you?

Quiet as a Mouse

Listening

Little ones are as quiet as the mouse in the story with this activity. Revisit the book, pointing out to students how the little mouse uses body language to communicate with the narrator. Ask youngsters a question such as "Do you like spinach?" or "How old are you?" Have them respond to the question using body language, such as facial expressions and gestures. Ask students several more questions, encouraging them to answer using different types of body language.

Searching for Strawberries

Math

In this activity, youngsters pretend to be the bear looking for strawberries. Make a class supply of strawberry cutouts and write a different number on each so the cutouts can be arranged in numerical order. Then hide the cutouts in your classroom. To begin, instruct students to pretend they are bears. Have them each find one strawberry and then return to their seats. Next, have the student with the strawberry numbered 1 stand in front of the class. Then have the student with the strawberry numbered 2 stand beside the first student. Continue in this manner until all the students are standing in order.

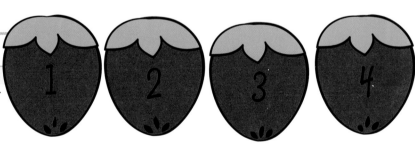

A Crafty Disguise

Art

The little mouse disguises the strawberry so the big hungry bear will not recognize it. Little ones create a disguise for their own strawberries with this quick-to-prepare project. Give each student a strawberry cutout and access to a variety of art materials, such as paper scraps, pom-poms, sequins, ribbons, markers, crayons, and glue. Have her glue the materials of her choice on the strawberry to create a disguise for it. Invite her to share her cleverly disguised strawberry with the class.

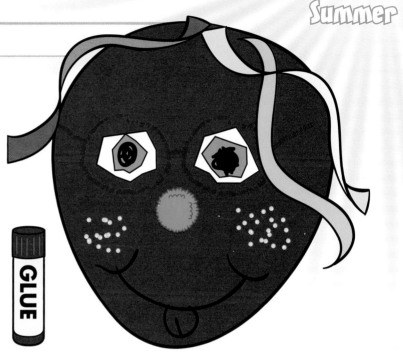

Quincy

The ice cream is best. It tastes good!

"Berry" Delicious Treats

Writing

In the story, the little mouse and the narrator share a fresh juicy strawberry, but there are many other ways to enjoy strawberries. Find out your little ones' favorites with this activity. Gather fresh strawberries along with a few other strawberry-flavored foods, such as jelly, cream cheese, yogurt, ice cream, or gelatin. Give each student a plate with a small sampling of each food. Invite him to taste each food and choose the one he likes best. On a sheet of paper, instruct him to draw the food he likes best and write or dictate a sentence about his drawing.

Blueberries for Sal

Written and illustrated by Robert McCloskey

Little Sal and her mother go to Blueberry Hill to pick blueberries. Little Bear and his mother go to Blueberry Hill to eat blueberries. When Little Sal and Little Bear wander off and then trail after the wrong mothers, there are hilarious results!

Little Sal — Little Bear

Little Sal
- is a human
- wears shoes and clothes
- rides in a car
- lives in a house

(center)
- like blueberries
- have mothers
- get lost

Little Bear
- is an animal
- has fur
- lives in a cave

Let's Compare!

Literacy

Little Sal and Little Bear both like blueberries even though the little girl and the little bear are quite different. Prompt little ones to think of more similarities and differences between Little Sal and Little Bear with this activity. Draw a Venn diagram on your board and label it as shown. Then ask students to share ways that Little Sal and Little Bear are different. Write the information in the appropriate sections of the diagram. Next, have little ones describe how Sal and the bear are the same. Write youngsters' suggestions in the middle of the diagram.

A Bucket of Berries

Art

Kuplunk! Sal plops her tasty blueberries in a metal pail. Encourage youngsters to make a pail just like Sal's with this fun art project. Have each child glue pieces of aluminum foil to a tagboard pail cutout. Help her fold any overlapping edges of foil to the back of the cutout. Next, encourage her to glue the pail to a sheet of paper. Have her make blue fingerprints at the top of the pail and around the bottom of the pail. Little Sal sure has collected a lot of blueberries!

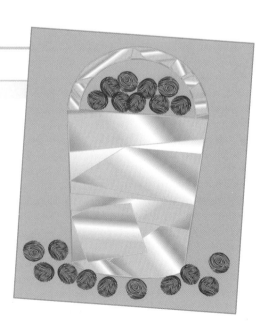

Thud, Bonk, Plink!

Science

When Sal put blueberries in her bucket, they went "kuplink, kuplank, kuplunk!" Students will be eager to hear noises other items make when dropped in a pail! Gather several classroom objects and a metal pail. Have students listen carefully as a different volunteer drops each item into the pail. Invite students to describe the noises made by the objects. Next, have youngsters cover their eyes as you drop one of the items into the pail. Have students uncover their eyes. Then invite youngsters to guess which item was dropped in the pail. Continue in the same way with the remaining items.

Counting Berries

Math

The pail in this center will be full of berries, just as Sal's mother's pail was in the story. Place a pail and a container of blue pom-poms (blueberries) at a center along with a large foam die. Two youngsters visit the center. A youngster rolls the die, counts the corresponding number of blueberries, and then places the blueberries in the pail. If desired, encourage her to say "kuplink, kuplank, kuplunk" as she adds the berries. Have her partner repeat the process. Students continue in the same way until the pail is full of berries.

Down by the Bay

Illustrated by Nadine Bernard Westcott

This book shows eye-catching illustrations to match the traditional song "Down by the Bay," a toe-tapping nonsense song that highlights silly rhymes.

Watermelon Patch

Math

There's a bumper crop of watermelons down by the bay. With this counting activity, there will be a crop of watermelons in your classroom as well! Label separate sheets of paper with watermelon vines and different numbers. Place large green pom-poms in a container. Then gather youngsters around the props. Invite a child to choose a paper and name the number. Next, have a second volunteer place the appropriate number of watermelons on the paper as the remaining students count along. Continue in the same way until each paper has the correct number of watermelons.

Silly Rhymes

Literacy

In the story, there's a fly wearing a tie and a bear combing its hair. No doubt youngsters will be eager to make up their own silly rhymes with a new cast of critters. In advance, cut out a copy of the cards on page 127 and place them in a bag. Review the rhymes in the story. Then have a child choose a card from the bag and attach it to a sheet of chart paper. Help students make up a rhyme for the animal similar to the rhymes in the story; then write the students' words on the paper. Continue in the same way for each remaining card.

Did you ever see a cat wearing a hat?

Did you ever see a goat with a sore throat?

Did you ever see a bug drinking from a mug?

Watermelon Parfait

Listening

With all those watermelons growing down by the bay, youngsters are sure to be eager for a watermelon-flavored snack! In advance, make batches of watermelon-flavored gelatin and lime-flavored gelatin and obtain a container of whipped topping. Place the ingredients at a table along with disposable cups and spoons. Invite youngsters to the table and tell each student to place a spoonful of lime gelatin in a cup, then a spoonful of watermelon gelatin, and last, a dollop of whipped cream. Then have her assemble and eat her snack.

Polka-Dot Tails

Art

These polka-dot whale tales look lovely on a bulletin board. Place bingo daubers, sticky dots, and hole-punched dots at a table along with glue and a class supply of construction paper whale tails. A youngster decorates her whale tail with dots until a desired effect in achieved. Attach the finished tail to a bulletin board decorated with ocean waves. Then title the board "Did You Ever See Whales With Polka-Dot Tails?"

Fish Eyes:
A Book You Can Count On

Written and illustrated by Lois Ehlert

A little black fish explores a sea of colorful friends in this counting extravaganza! The clever cutout eyes of the fish he meets and the subtle addition skills incorporated into the story make this book appealing for all.

A Fish Wish

Literacy

The little black fish sees oodles of lovely colorful fish in the sea. Ask youngsters what color fish they would prefer to be with this fun rhyme. Place colorful fish cutouts on the floor. Choose a child and then recite the rhyme shown. Encourage the child to choose the fish she prefers and then name its color. Have her place the fish back on the floor. Then continue in the same way with different youngsters.

If you could wish
To be a fish,
What color would you be,
Little fishy in the sea?

Shapely Fish

Art

With this art project, youngsters make fish that closely resemble the fish in Ms. Ehlert's illustrations. In advance, cut out a variety of colorful triangles. Place the triangles at a table along with glue, sticky dots, hole-punched dots, and sheets of blue construction paper. A child glues triangles to the paper so they resemble fish and then attaches dots to the fish to make eyes.

Fish Eyes: A Book You Can Count On

Move Like a Fish

Gross motor

The fish in the story jump and dart! Invite little ones to move as the fish do with this simple musical activity. Review with students the ways that the fish move in the story, helping youngsters understand that the word *darting* means moving suddenly and quickly. Have students name other ways that fish move. Then prompt youngsters to demonstrate different movements. Next, play a recording of upbeat music and have students move about the room like fish.

What Colorful Eyes!

Math

Have youngsters notice the eye cutouts in the story and how the color of each fish's eye depends on the color of the page directly behind the fish. Give each youngster a fish cutout and have her use a hole puncher to give it an eye. Have students sit in your large-group area with their fish in their hands. Say, "Give your fish a blue eye." Then have each child find something blue in the classroom and place her fish against the object so the blue shows through the eyehole. After checking to make sure each child found the correct color, repeat the activity with a different color.

Swimmy

Written and illustrated by Leo Lionni

How will a school of fish frolic in the sea when big hungry fish are lurking about? Swimmy has the answer! He gathers all of his fish friends into a school shaped like an enormous fish!

Question Fish

Literacy

Little ones select fish to reveal questions for them to answer about the story. In advance, write questions, such as those shown, on separate red fish cutouts. Place the red fish in a bag along with several blank black fish cutouts. Have a child choose a fish. If he chooses a red fish, read aloud the question and then have students answer it, referring back to the book as needed. If a youngster chooses a black fish, have youngsters say, "Swimmy!" as they stand and pretend to swim. Repeat the process until all the fish have been removed from the bag.

Questions

How is Swimmy different from his brothers and sisters?
What ate the school of little red fish?
How did Swimmy feel after his brothers and sisters were eaten?
What kinds of creatures did Swimmy see in the ocean?
Why was the second school of red fish hiding?
What did Swimmy do so the fish could swim safely?
What part of the big fish did Swimmy become?

The Hungry Tuna

Math

A hungry tuna eats an entire school of red fish. Your youngsters are sure to enjoy feeding this tuna to practice their counting skills. Attach two black disposable plates to each other and then cut a mouth opening through both plates as shown. Attach triangles to the opposite side of the plates so they resemble a tail. Then attach eye cutouts to the project. Make a supply of red fish cutouts. Have a child roll a large die and count the dots. Then have the remaining youngsters count aloud as the child counts fish and places them in the tuna's mouth. Repeat the process several times.

Fish Snack

Literacy

Have little ones revisit the story with a snack that looks similar to Swimmy and his friends! Give each child a cup containing orange fish-shaped crackers and one fish-shaped cracker in a different color. Also give each child a sheet of paper with an outline drawing of a fish. Have each child arrange the crackers in the outline so the crackers resemble Swimmy and his friends forming the large fish. Ask youngsters to explain what happened in the story. Then invite students to nibble on their snacks.

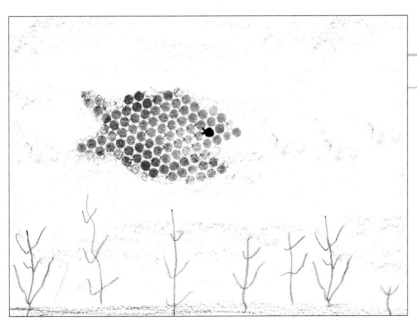

A Printmaking Project

Art

Youngsters add details to Bubble Wrap cushioning material prints to make a scene from the story. In advance, trim a piece of large Bubble Wrap cushioning material into the shape of a fish. Have a child color a sheet of white construction paper with unwrapped blue crayons. Next, encourage a youngster to paint the prepared cushioning material red and then make a print on the paper. When the paint dries, have her use a fine-tip black marker to color one of the bubble prints black so it resembles Swimmy. Then encourage her to use fine-tip markers to add fin details to the print.

A House for Hermit Crab

Written and illustrated by Eric Carle

After Hermit Crab realizes that his shell is too snug, he moves to a larger shell. Over time, he decorates the new shell and makes it a perfect home. When Hermit Crab outgrows that shell as well, he learns that moving can be both sad and exciting.

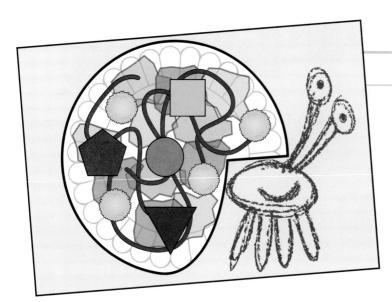

Decorate a Shell

Art

Little ones can decorate a shell to look like Hermit Crab's with this simple project. Give each child a paper plate trimmed as shown. Have her glue the plate to a sheet of construction paper. Then have her draw the hermit crab's head and legs on the paper. Next, invite her to glue craft items to the shell to represent all the friends Hermit Crab picks up in his travels.

Small to Large

Math

Whenever Hermit Crab's shell gets too tight, he discards the old shell and finds a bigger one. With this activity, invite students to put Hermit Crab's discarded shells in order by size. Have each child color and cut out a copy of page 128. Then encourage her to order the shells from small to large on a 6" x 18" strip of construction paper. When you have checked to make sure the shells are in size order, have her glue her shells to the strip.

A House for Hermit Crab

January to December
Literacy

Have little ones place the months of the year in order throughout Hermit Crab's journey. Laminate large month cards. Then read aloud each card and give each one to a different student. Next, reread the story, prompting each child to place his card on the floor at the appropriate time to make a path of cards. When the story is finished, tape the resulting path to the floor. Then prompt each child to hop on the month cards as you help her recite the months.

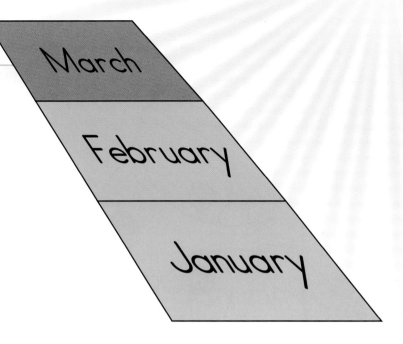

A Searching Song
Literacy

Youngsters find the perfect home for Hermit Crab with this fun song and game. In advance, place a class supply of seashells or seashell cutouts around the room. Lead youngsters in singing the song shown below several times as they search for the seashells. When each child has found a seashell, have him place it in your circle-time area. Then gather youngsters around the seashells. Have students discuss which shell they believe would be the best home for a hermit crab. If desired, have students sort the seashells by size and then re-sort them by type.

(sung to the tune of "My Bonnie Lies Over the Ocean")

A hermit crab's home is a seashell.
He takes his home with him each day.
But when it gets too small to live in,
He finds a new home right away.
Searching, searching,
He's searching to find a new home, a home!
Searching, searching,
He's searching to find a new home!

Raccoon Pattern
Use with "Night School" on page 5.

TEC61181

The _____ Tree

My favorite treat made from

apples is _____.

by _____

Squirrel Pattern

Use with "Adorable Squirrel" on page 16.

TEC61181

Growing Pumpkins

Name _____

Seasonal Storytime • ©The Mailbox® Books • TEC61181

Pick big pumpkins.

Make jack-o'-lanterns.

Watch them grow.

Plant the seeds.

Scarecrow Patterns
Use with "Noisy Items" on page 24 and "Knock, Knock!" on page 25.

TEC61181

TEC61181

TEC61181

TEC61181

TEC61181

TEC61181

Seasonal Storytime • ©The Mailbox® Books • TEC61181

TEC61181

TEC61181

Critter Patterns
Use with "Turkey Search" on page 26.

TEC61181

TEC61181

TEC61181

TEC61181

TEC61181

Picture Cards
Use with "A Greedy Guest" and "A Little Old Lady Balloon" on page 28.

TEC61181

TEC61181

TEC61181

TEC61181

TEC61181

TEC61181

TEC61181

TEC61181

TEC61181

Seasonal Storytime • ©The Mailbox® Books • TEC61181

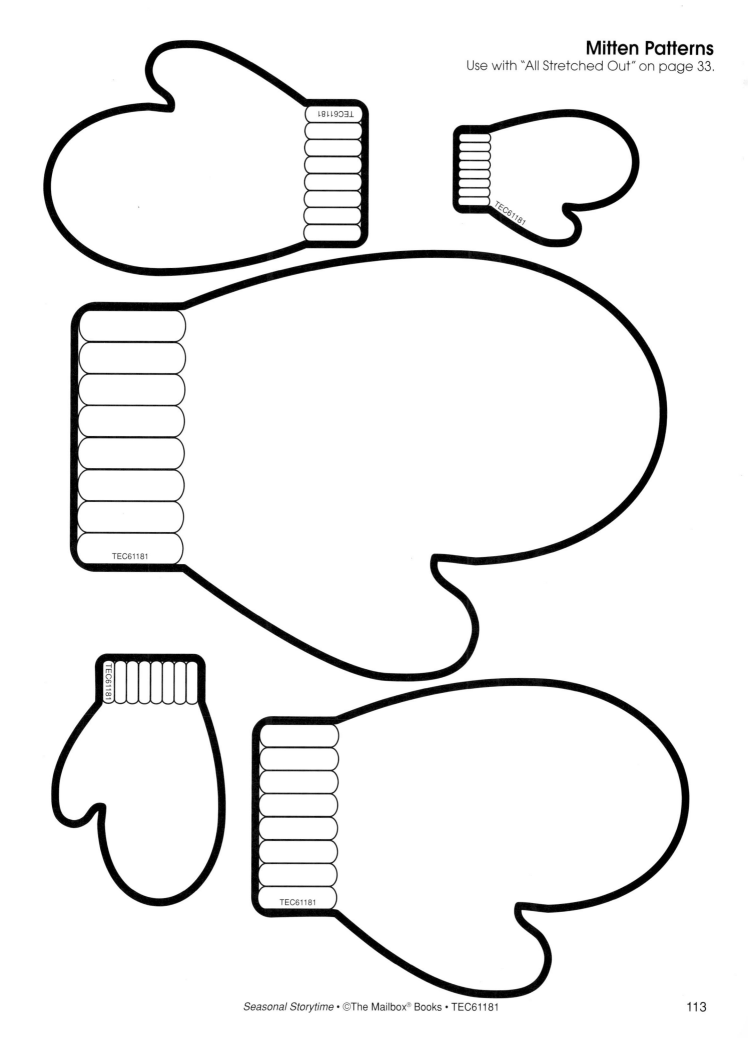

TEC61181

TEC61181

TEC61181

TEC61181

TEC61181

The hedgehog's _____ will keep it warm.

Seasonal Storytime • ©The Mailbox® Books • TEC61181

114   **Note to the teacher:** Use with "Dressed for the Weather" on page 34.

Mouse and Hare popped white corn and brewed black tea.

Note to the teacher: Use with "Popcorn and Tea" on page 36.

Animal Cards
Use with "Party Animals" on page 37.

TEC61181

TEC61181

TEC61181

TEC61181

TEC61181

TEC61181

TEC61181

TEC61181

Gingerbread House Pattern

Use with "From Place to Place" and "Home, Sweet Home" on page 38 and "In, Out, and All Around" on page 39.

TEC61181

Gingerbread Baby Patterns

Use with "From Place to Place" and "Home, Sweet Home" on page 38 and "In, Out, and All Around" on page 39.

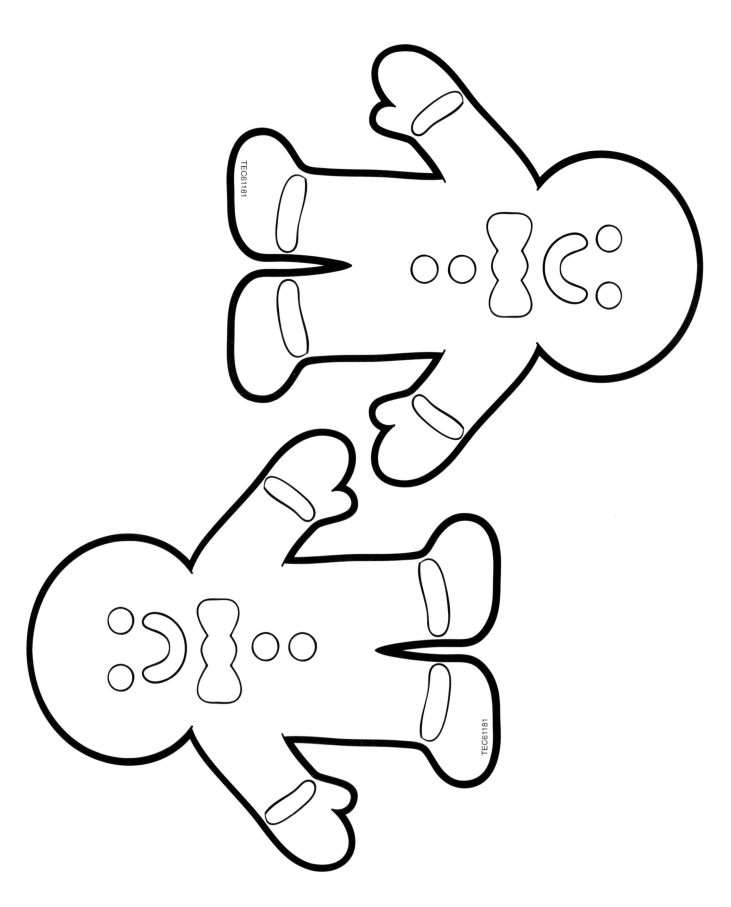

 Seasonal Storytime • ©The Mailbox® Books • TEC61181

Ice-Skating

Making Snow Angels

Having Races

Playing Baseball

Sledding

Having a Snowball Fight

Menorah Pattern
Use with "A Marvelous Menorah" on page 47.

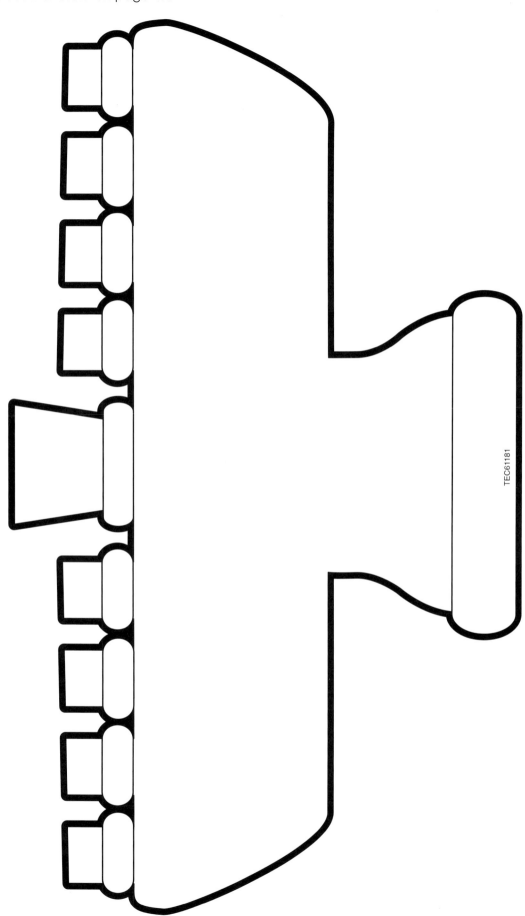

TEC61181

TEC61181

Story Strips

Use with "Pop-Up Story Prop" on page 56.

TEC61181

TEC61181

TEC61181

Oh-oh! Grass!

TEC61181

Oh-oh! A river!

TEC61181

Oh-oh! Mud!

TEC61181

Oh-oh! A forest!

TEC61181

Oh-oh! A snowstorm!

TEC61181

Oh-oh! A cave!

TEC61181

Animal Patterns
Use with "Bath Time" and "In the Tub" on page 77.

TEC61181

TEC61181

TEC61181

TEC61181

TEC61181

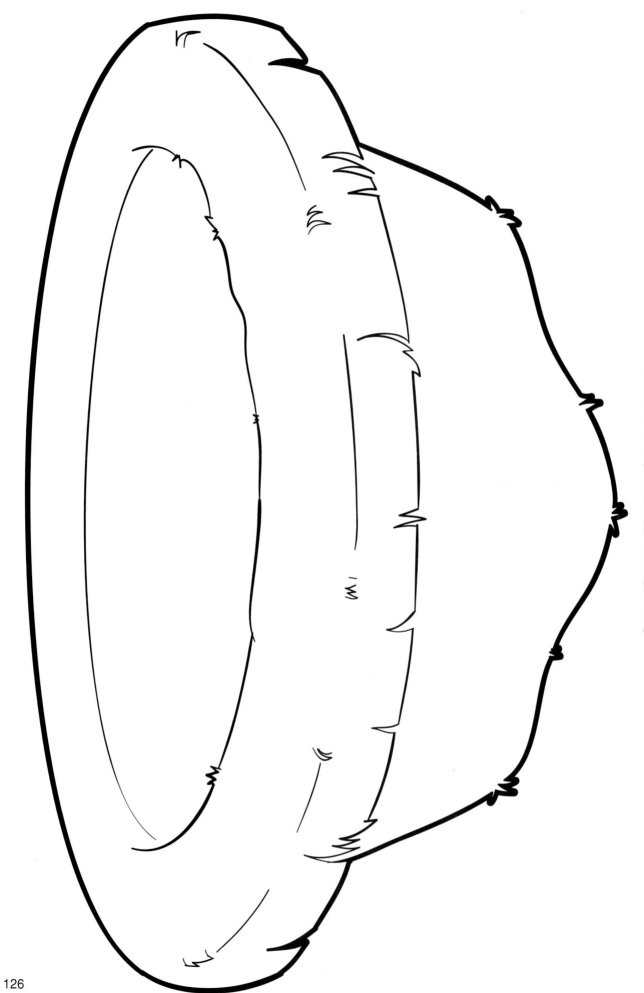

Seasonal Storytime • ©The Mailbox® Books • TEC61181

Note to the teacher: Use with "Hat Full of Berries" on page 90 and "Count and Chant" on page 91.

TEC61181

TEC61181

TEC61181

TEC61181

TEC61181

TEC61181

Shell Cards

Use with "Small to Large" on page 102.

TEC61181